INTO THE MA

Nicci Gerrard is a freelance journalist living in London. She co-founded *Women's Review* in 1985 and was co-editor until its demise two years later. She now writes regularly for *The Observer* and *New Statesman and Society*. She lives with journalist Colin Hughes and their two small children.

into the
MAINSTREAM

Nicci Gerrard

London   Boston   Sydney   Wellington

First published by Pandora Press, an imprint of the Trade Division of
Unwin Hyman, in 1989.

PANDORA PRESS
Unwin Hyman Limited
15/17 Broadwick Street
London W1V 1FP

Unwin Hyman Inc.
8 Winchester Place, Winchester, MA 01890

Allen & Unwin Australia Pty Ltd
P.O. Box 764, 8 Napier Street, North Sydney, NSW 2060

Allen & Unwin NZ Ltd (in association with the Port Nicholson Press)
Compusales Building, 75 Ghuznee Street, Wellington, New Zealand

British Library Cataloguing in Publication Data

Gerrard, Nicci.
Into the mainstream: how feminism has
changed women's writing.
I. Title
820′.9′9287

ISBN 0–04–440366–6

Typeset by Computape (Pickering) Ltd, North Yorkshire
Printed in Great Britain by
Cox & Wyman Ltd., Reading

For Colin

CONTENTS

CONTENTS

ACKNOWLEDGMENTS

Thanks to the following writers, editors, critics and literary agents to whom I talked during the course of writing the book: Kathy Anderson, Deborah Baker, Leland Bardwell, Sally Beauman, Philippa Brewster, Catherine Brophy, Rebecca Brown, Antonia Byatt, Liz Calder, Mary Clemmy, Mary Cunnane, Gill Davies, Anita Desai, Leslie Dick, Mary Dorcey, Maureen Duffy, Andrea Dworkin, Zoë Fairbairns, Elaine Feinstein, Alison Fell, Penelope Fitzgerald, Marilyn French, Maggie Gee, Elaine Gill, Anne Godoff, Graham Greene, Elizabeth Hardwick, Keri Hulme, Mary Paul Keane, Ros de Lanerolle, Frances Goldin, Mary Lavin, Elspeth Lindner, Anne McDermid, Shena Mackay, Sara Maitland, Sue Miller, Kate Mosse, Joyce Carol Oates, Ursula Owen, Ros Parr, Marge Piercy, Joan Riley, Michèle Roberts, Elaine Showalter, Mona Simpson, Dale Spender, Meredith Tax, Emma Tennant, Mindy Werner, Barbara Wilson, Jeanette Winterson.

I am especially grateful to my editor Candida Lacey, who made the difficult partnership between editor and author seem easy with her patience, friendly criticisms and intellectual clarity; to all those who worked with me on *Women's Review* until its end; to my parents for their encouragement and freezer meals, and my whole family for their constant support; to Claire for Wednesdays; to my little son Edgar who made me realise the joys and horrors confronting many women writers who are also mothers; and to Colin Hughes for his sanity and unstinting generosity.

INTRODUCTION

——————

I believe we must cope courageously and practically, as women have always done, with the here and now, our feet on this ground where we now live. But nothing less than the most radical imagination will carry us beyond this place, beyond the mere struggle for survival, to that lucid recognition of our possibilities which will keep us impatient and unresigned to mere survival.
Adrienne Rich, from *On Lies, Secrets and Silence*

In order for the artist to have a world to express, he/she must first be situated in this world, oppressed or oppressing, resigned or rebellious . . .
Simone de Beauvoir, from *The Ethics of Ambiguity*

All fiction is rooted in experience. However it is subsequently shaped by the imagination, it is born from the particular life of its author, and grows from its particular culture. Most works of fiction remain stubbornly within their narrow worlds: either they are forgotten as that world disappears, or they are remembered as socially interesting relics. Written from their time and about their time, they are creations of their time. They are novels that respond to and reveal the symptoms of an age, reflecting back to the reader the context in which she or he lives. But a few works of fiction see beyond the symptoms. They diagnose an age and even

1

seek to change it. Such novels possess the imaginative power and speculative intelligence that transform experience into enduring fictions. Rooted in the here and now, they give us imaginary worlds that lift us, to borrow Adrienne Rich's words, 'beyond this place'.

If all fiction is rooted in its own culture, then all fiction is, in a wide and vague sense, 'political'. But there is a gulf between the novel whose ideological line is so undigested that it makes its fiction into a hasty scaffolding and its reader into an unparticipating pupil, and the work that seeks to understand and alchemise the political and cultural complexities of its world. Ann Petry wrote that 'all truly great art is propaganda'. Novels which survive their time seed their imagined worlds in the consciousness of their readers.

Of course, some ages seem to throw up an extraordinary number of writers of stature, by somehow providing fertile soil for the creative imagination. Two decades have passed since the rebirth of the women's movement. Just as feminism has come of age, so too has the writing that grew up under its wing. Feminist literature has entered the mainstream of the 1980s. Entering the mainstream holds a host of opposing interpretations: selling, or selling out; gaining access, or losing substance; making more money, or taking fewer risks; becoming part of the larger world, or relinquishing the female world. It is 'coping practically and courageously' with the world in which we live, and it is weakly swimming with the tide. It implies success to some and failure to others. Like all main streams, the waters are impure – and some women may long to return to the tributary days. But it is futile to feel nostalgic regret for the dramatic certainties of feminism's beginning. We have to live in today's muddy anxieties.

The materialism and legitimised greed of the 1980s, its spurious nostalgia and conservatism, do not make it into a particularly inspiring decade for writers in either the United Kingdom or the United States. Its culture of consumerism, unapologetic philistinism and its ethos of individual survival opposes many of the standards that our most enduring literature upholds. And yet it is also a decade in which women writers,

2

supported by an anxious but established feminism, encouraged by their forerunners of the 1950s and 1960s, enabled by the birth of so many women's presses, and increasingly recognised and sought after by the general public, could be expected to triumph. Have they risen above a passionless decade to give us works of real passion and intellectual vitality? Or have they been sucked into that decade? Influenced by the swift advances and faltering steps of contemporary feminism, how have women writers then shaped, and been shaped by, their culture?

The 1980s can seem both a crucial pivot between two symbolically powerful ages – in Britain in particular it is hard not to believe that something has irrevocably changed – and a waiting time. The year 2000, as we approach it, feels simultaneously to be a culmination and a beginning – a fearful anticipation of history coming to an end, and of the future finally being disclosed. The late 1960s and the 1970s remain potent reminders, for many, of heady dreams and illusions. They are decades that promised a better future, yet failed to deliver it; they are also decades that, for women in particular, nurtured ideals. The final years of the twentieth century are likely to be pervaded by a sense of approaching climax and of lost faith. In the literature that is being written by women, that atmosphere is reproduced in diverse, sometimes devious, ways. Meanwhile in the 1980s, there has been a feeling of transition; and in the literature of the 1980s there is often a sense of contradictory impulses. The drabness of the decade, its cultural greyness, moral ambivalence and apathy, has a swelling undertow of moral urgency. We do not live in a literary desert. If rampant materialism and defensive individualism have impoverished our cultures, there are signs nonetheless of a creative upheaval and revival amid the apathy and uncertainty. Women writers are not merely waiting between the acts.

1968 has by now acquired the satisfying clarity and alluring sheen of memory. Many women who vote, work, and lead active political and emotional lives are not old enough to recall the year; many others did not experience it directly at the time. It has become an icon in socialist and feminist history, a Golden

Age and a convenient landmark of change. Nostalgia has converted its confusions into certainties, its anger into heroic drama and its optimism into betrayed faith.

Nevertheless, something significant did happen then. Many people who participated believed that life could never be the same again. Hundreds of thousands felt the impact more gently. The hopes and theories that crystallised during that year were clarified, refined and worked upon: they filtered down over the years, laying the foundations of modern feminism. Disrespect for the establishment, faith in the power of the powerless individual, a vision of a better and more peaceful world, anger on behalf of those underprivileged, mistreated and dispossessed, all collided in a summer of active disruption, sparking off the 'sixties revolution'. It was a heady revolution for many, and quickly acquired the seductive symbols and theatricality of a young and flamboyant, visible and articulate, counterculture – therapy and consciousness-raising, love-ins and pacifism, long dresses and long hair and cultivated gentleness of speech, youth culture and flower power, sexual freedom and political anger.

But for others it was a destructive and illusory revolution. Sexual freedom often meant sexual freedom for *men*; anti-materialism often meant an alternative kind of greed. Love could easily be a profound narcissism, and high ideals an empty and complacent rhetoric. The young of 1968 are now approaching middle age. In the late 1980s, many of them are apolitical or vote Conservative, have discarded hippie-dom for yuppie-dom, and feel embarrassed affection for the naive youths they once were. Grown-up, they now understand that Utopias describe only current desires, not future possibilities.

Although 1968 and its aftermath did bring about changes, it is for many of us, too young to remember it clearly, more potent and enduring as a symbol. But it is precisely the popular interpretation of that heady summer as an impossible dream which robs it of any enduring power and replaces its political implications with a facile nostalgia.

The one enduring political movement which grew out of it, and on from it, was the women's liberation movement. The events of that year were valuable lessons for another kind of revolution. The power of the individual and the effectiveness of the collective, the perception of the ways in which gender-related issues can unite women of different ages and backgrounds, the growing awareness of how public and political life has an effect on every aspect of personal life, all became cornerstones of feminism.

It is many years now since we have been able to talk of a single and unified entity called 'the women's movement'. Not since the fierce disagreements which broke up the national conference of 1978 have there been gatherings of the entire movement. There has been a gradual withering away of unified campaigns and organisations. Feminism is now so fragmented and dispersed that it is hard to perceive any sense of a common purpose. The original demands of the women's movement were for equal pay, equal education and job opportunities, free contraception, abortion on demand, 24-hour nurseries, legal and financial independence, an end to discrimination against lesbians and the right of all women to define their own sexuality, and freedom from intimidation by threat or use of violence or sexual coercion, regardless of marital status. These goals have not been achieved, but they were practical, clear-cut and generally agreed upon. Nowadays, it would be difficult to draw up a list of common aims.

By the end of the 1970s, the women's liberation movement had been fragmented over issues of race and especially sexuality. Fiercely opposing attitudes to heterosexuality and male violence shattered any hope of a common direction and, if not unity, at least a supportive coalition of women under the umbrella of the liberation movement. Lesbianism symbolised women's right to an autonomous sexuality, and lesbians were justly resentful of heterosexual women's complacent assumptions. Radical feminism grew out of the developing rift between women, and heterosexuality was explicitly articulated by some as the root cause of female oppression.

The emerging differences between socialist and cultural feminists can be traced in the feminist writing of the time – many of the separatist feminists came to see gender differences as innate, biological and inevitable; women, they argued, are *innately* superior to men. Socialist feminists saw oppression as socially constructed and comprehensive – a product of capitalism. The 'female writing' and the 'writing with the body' that flourished at the end of the 1970s and the beginning of the 1980s (Hélène Cixous, Mary Daly, Susan Griffin *et al.*) made femaleness into a separate, and intrinsically better, realm. Socialist feminists countered with analyses of exploitative practices and cultural constructs, arguing that women are not better than men – they have simply been denied the power to be powerfully destructive. But socialist feminists tended to concentrate so much upon the public world of work that they often ignored women's private worlds – or neglected the powerful and positive sides of motherhood and femaleness. When radical feminists rejected the mainstream, equating it with *malestream*, they were also rejecting socialist feminist – or 'integrationist feminist' – theory. It was a bitter polarisation of women who had set out together to achieve 'liberation'.

So, within two decades, the women's liberation movement became 'feminism', entering the vocabulary of most people but relinquishing its distinct identity. The dramatic certainties of feminism in the early 1970s, the ways in which women were converted to it, empowered by it and had their world illuminated by it, can now make contemporary feminism seem a pale and limping ghost of its former self. Where once it was fired by faith in a feminist future, now it is on the defensive against a backlash. Where once there was a feeling, however ill-based, of solidarity between women of different classes and races, now schisms have developed. Where once the women's movement presented a threat to the establishment, now its bowdlerised ideas have been cosily absorbed so that in Britain the right-wing ex-junior health minister, Edwina Currie, can call herself a feminist and Margaret Thatcher can use its vocabulary without blinking. The 'independent woman' has become an advertising slogan and a consumer target.

The splits, bitter arguments and developing factions were

inevitable. Now we have radical feminists, separatist feminists, Christian feminists, social feminists, Marxist feminists, New Wave Feminists, post-feminist feminists and the 'I'm-not-a-feminist-but . . .' feminists. As the movement grew, it was bound to lose the intimacy and familial atmosphere of its earliest days. As theories and priorities were developed, there was bound to be disagreement – and sometimes violent disagreement. By the end of the 1970s and the early 1980s there was a kind of frictional diversity which, if sometimes bruising to individuals and lacerating to the women's movement's reputation, was nevertheless vital, committed and robust.

Fragmentation can, in theory, pave the way for increased pluralism and cultural diversity, becoming a kind of creative chaos. And argument is always more optimistic – because more committed – than indifference. But in the late 1980s it is indifference that has become the creeping danger that lurks around fragmented feminisms, and around the general position of women. Apathy has set in. A newly coined and chilling little word is in circulation: post-feminism. Post-feminism implies that feminism has done its job and is over. It includes feminism in its coinage but simultaneously denies it. It interprets feminism as a tool with which women have achieved certain ends, rather than an ever-evolving and dynamic process. It is a largely media-created concept, but is rooted in fact, and recognisable in form.

Post-feminists are a product of the 1980s and are said to be quite different from pre-feminists: they are the fall-out from the fragments. For them, there are as many feminisms as there are feminists – and so the word's meaning implodes. So-called post-feminists believe fiercely in individual equality, making full use of the freedoms won for them by previous generations, and usually behaving in an assertive, stylish and self-possessed manner. Their position is not political but anti-political – they have discarded the collective spirit for a liberated individualism. They would fight for their own rights and against manifest sexual prejudice, but they would not organise to fight for the rights of all women. In contrast to the new generation of self-confident and aspiring women – Thatcher's children, who have never voted in an election not won by her and can hardly remember a time when she was not leader of the Conservative Party – the older generation of feminists can appear old-fashioned, woolly, idealistic and unstylish. Their concern with the political aspects of tiny personal details (the shaved-leg debate, worrying about wearing clothes that give out the 'right' message . . .) is dismissed by younger women as puritanical or trivial. Feminism, once regarded as radical and charged with excitement, now appears tedious to many – a has-been.

Feminism in both Britain and the United States is not only under attack from expected opponents; it is also receiving only meagre support from parts of its natural constituency. Margaret Thatcher in Britain, or Ronald Reagan and George Bush in the United States, have appealed not just to individual greed or facile nostalgia, but to the desire that almost every one of us has for comfort, security and moral simplicity in an increasingly uncomfortable and uncertain world.

Within such a culture feminism has tended to retreat from the front line of change. In the first flush of youth it was certain, uncompromising, disruptive, exciting and challenging; its radical theories explored social structures. In the tentative years of its transition from adolescence to maturity, and from fringe to mainstream, it has become a clarifying, organising and consolidating movement – less innovative and ambitious, but more accessible; more generally accepted, but less progressive and less fired by dramatic truths and passionate convictions.

Much literature which influences and is influenced by feminism is undergoing the same process of necessary but frequently uninspiring consolidation and clarification. Rather than responding to a small-spirited and materialistic age with big-hearted and adventurous urgency, it has adopted a largely defensive position: reiterating old truths, returning to familiar themes, remaining within the feminist literary tradition of the 1970s, writing personal confessional novels about individual lives.

Many women believed that feminism, in radically restructuring the society in which we live, would herald an equivalent literary transformation. There are ways in which it did fundamentally alter the literary landscape. Feminism gave birth to women's presses. In Britain, The Women's Press, Pandora, Virago, Sheba and Onlywomen Press encouraged women to write about their particular female experience, and inspired women to read books that gave them a female perspective on the world. In North America it encouraged mainstream presses to take on feminist books and series. It legitimised subjects for fiction which previously had been regarded as trivial. It was exciting, new, subversive and challenging, and it produced exciting new writers. Then, too, it felt important for books of analysis and novels to explore with detail and realism how women conducted their lives. Feminist writers were vital to the liberation movement. The politics of personal experience were crucial in changing women's positions in the world. Reading Marge Piercy or Germaine Greer, Kate Millett, Adrienne Rich or Betty Friedan illuminated for many women how the nitty-gritty of their lives meant something beyond itself. It had a political content. But that was in the 1970s. Truths too often reiterated take on the tone of platitudes.

In Britain, those women's presses which have sprung up over the last two decades have not only introduced women's writing to readers who were hungry for it, and provided space for writers from different backgrounds and cultures, they have also formed a pressure group upon the mainstream houses. Virago was one of the first publishing houses to introduce the trade paperback – which took off against predictions and was swiftly taken up by the larger presses. The commitment of Sheba and The Women's Press to black, third-world and working-class women led the way for an increased general interest in marginalised writers. Onlywomen Press introduced lesbian writers who could not find publishers in the mainstream. But in the last years of the 1980s the radicalism and independence of women's presses have been threatened by the takeover boom in the publishing world. Increasingly, the energies of the women's presses and women writers are directed into clarification and popularisation. The teenage and young adult series, the detective and science fiction novels, the general interest explanations of feminist thought (sophisticated versions of 'how to' books) are necessary moves towards integration. But they are not at the cutting edge of feminism. The anxious feminist debate between selling and selling out, accessibility and over-dilution, is reflected in what is now being published.

Above all, in the women's movement of the past decades, there was the sense of choice and space in which to operate. At times that led to slackness – I spoke to editors who recall simply 'receiving' manuscripts which, if they were competent and of the right length, were almost bound to be published. But it also led to a form of cultural possibility which has since vanished. Gill Davies of Tavistock Press points to the recent tendency among academic writers and publishers to be 'practical' in what they write and publish. But the most exciting intellectual theories are often brought about by the impractical leaps of a freely hypothesising imagination. It is as if increased personal and institutional prosperity has been bought by tighter personal margins. The price that we pay for increasing wealth is less time and imaginative space; growth also implies shrinkage, and fewer connections between intellectual and political spheres. Without connections, there is no spark.

During the course of writing this book, I spoke to more than thirty editors and literary agents about the business of women's writing, and to more than fifty women writers about how and why they write, about the connections between the real world in which they live and the imaginary worlds they have created and about their political beliefs and literary ambitions. I asked them how they had been affected by feminism, whether they felt themselves to be 'feminist writers', and what they wanted their writing to achieve. I asked small questions of the 'do you use a word processor' and 'describe your working day' kind, and large abstract ones that sought to discover why women wrote what they did.

There were several writers, both in Great Britain and especially in North America, with whom I would have wished to have spoken but was, usually for geographical reasons, unable to – particularly several of the black American writers whose writing

10

has been of such vitality and significance in the 1980s. Nevertheless, I tried to talk to writers across a broad spectrum of ages, genres and backgrounds. I talked to writers of the older generation, who began to publish their work in the 1950s and early 1960s and who have had such an influence on their successors, such as Marge Piercy and Marilyn French from North America, Maureen Duffy, Elaine Feinstein, Emma Tennant and Antonia Byatt from England, and Mary Lavin from Ireland; to writers who experience marginalisation because of their race or sexual preference, like Joan Riley, Mary Dorcey, Jane Rule and Barbara Wilson; to first-time writers, like Leslie Dick, Rebecca Brown and Catherine Brophy; to explicitly feminist writers who were born out of the women's movement, such as Zoë Fairbairns, Michèle Roberts, Alison Fell and Sara Maitland; to newly established writers of great promise, such as Maggie Gee or Jeanette Winterson; to prolific writers such as Joyce Carol Oates; to outrageous and controversial writers, such as Andrea Dworkin, to writers from India (Anita Desai) and New Zealand (Keri Hulme); to writers of detective fiction and romance. I have also looked at the lives and writing of numerous other women: Margaret Drabble, Nadine Gordimer, Toni Morrison, Fay Weldon, Maya Angelou, Angela Carter, Gloria Naylor, Janet Frame, Anita Brookner, Doris Lessing, Margaret Atwood . . . I could not hope to be comprehensive, but I have attempted to raise some questions about the business of publishing, and the present and future of women's writing.

Of course, I received a great variety of responses. Some women welcomed the revolution in the world of publishing because it implied a greater investment in literature; others disliked its increased multinationalism and anonymity, seeing the way in which books are treated as products as a comment on the philistine 1980s. Some accepted the fact that they had to help promote their work by marketing their own personality, while others vigorously condemned the increasing importance of packaging and hype. Some women welcomed the label 'feminist writer'; more shrank from it as if it cast a death-wish upon their work. Some had a particular politics which they wanted to reproduce in their fiction; others condemned the proselytising character of many contemporary novels.

But I was struck by how many women shared common preoccupations and anxieties. Almost all of them acknowledged with gratitude the debt they felt to the women's movement; even those writers who firmly rejected the tag of 'feminist' recognised that their writing had been enabled and influenced by it. Most of those writers with whom I talked – particularly the British – attacked the culture from which and about which they wrote, seeing it as grey and passionless, intellectually dismissive and imaginatively repressive. Most of them expressed dismay with the fiction being produced in Britain and America – a fiction characterised by parochialism, caution or brittle trendiness. Above all, however – and here lay the note of hope for the future of women's writing – several women believed that they were writing at a moment of change which had enormous cultural and political possibilities, and that they had a moral task as writers to spearhead that change. Despite public indifference or even contempt, they persisted in seeing themselves as truth-tellers and soothsayers.

The women writers' belief in their importance in the politics and culture of their country may seem surprising, vainglorious and even naive – especially in a country like Britain, where intellectual debate is treated with deep suspicion, and where literature has been relegated to a form of decorative entertainment. In Nicaragua the revolution was led by poets; in Chile the poet Pablo Neruda has been directly involved in the fate of his country; in France writers influence government; even in the United States novelists can run for Senate. But in the United Kingdom, in the summer of 1988, a group of anti-Thatcherite writers who met at Lady Antonia Fraser's home to discuss their political role was ridiculed in the press. It seems almost an embarrassment – not quite in good taste – that writers should think they can *do* anything.

Novelists might want to *do* something, might want to be socially significant formers of cultural and political agendas – but it is hard for them to now find a suitable form for their large, contradictory and often chaotic anxieties. All the familiar genres seem exhausted and the familiar themes stale. It is here that the dispersed shards of feminism may hold out challenging literary, cultural and political possibilities. Feminist theories of deconstruction and psychoanalysis have denied absolute meaning, and undermined the authority of the word, allowing women in their fictions, as in life, to select and synthesise the pieces of an exploded tradition. Such validation of subjectivity can merely – and often does – herald a trendily irreverent and sloppily anarchic literary fashion. But, alchemised in the crucible of imagination and disciplined by painstaking craft, it can imply a freedom from the tyranny of a monolithic inheritance, a liberation from parochial concerns. It can conjure kaleidoscopic new possibilities.

On the whole, the most exciting, engaged and ambitious novels by women have deserted old literary traditions and have looted multiple genres, structures and styles, to create what Angela Carter calls a 'bricolage' effect. They have felt free to invent literary forms. Such novels – and there are not, as yet, many of them – have created their own context, fashioned their own truths, and plundered history, myth and future to invent new worlds for our imaginations.

It is these novels, rather than the explicitly ideological ones, which are 'political' and 'feminist' in the largest senses of the words. Very few of them are British. Most contemporary women writers have so far failed to respond with urgency to the sense of cultural crisis, or imaginatively to the imaginative hiatus. Angela Carter, who 'uses the whole of Western Europe as a scrapyard', is a rather lonely figure on the landscape, though approaching her are younger writers such as the audacious Jeanette Winterson. In North America the black American writers, like Toni Morrison, have also dared to take the whole world as their canvas. They may be exceptions – but they may be the forerunners in a feminist literary renaissance.

Women's writing, and feminist writing, is entering the mainstream – but that does not necessarily mean that it is discarding radical impulses for caution, nor that it is selling out. The integration is welcome precisely and paradoxically because it heralds a more genuinely radical direction – a broadening out from the literature of personal angst and domestic oppression. It is a painfully tentative and sporadic movement, but many feminist novels are leaving behind the brave and self-indulgent descriptions of individual suffering, in which pain is worn like a badge of moral superiority. Instead, they are increasingly exploratory and ambitious. They are more political, because they are in motion; more inventive because they are not confined by static, predetermined theories, which have tended to transfix the imagination. They are more feminist, because less policed by a repressive feminist ideology; more illuminating because the novel's spotlight casts a wider arc. And they are more mainstream because, quite simply, they are more enjoyable.

o n e

LITERATURE'S PROFIT AND LOSS

The sense of cultural crisis in Britain today is expressed in often contradictory ways. Intellectuals point out that we are an anti-intellectual country; artists and writers complain that we are both increasingly philistine and yet elitist. Opposition politicians talk of the culture of materialism; Conservative politicians raise comsumerism into a proud Tory credo, while lamenting the failure of moral and spiritual values. Many of us feel a less specific but more pervasive sense of cultural malaise. Its most recognisable form is apathy. The lack of passion is neatly expressed by the use of old 1960s songs, which once captured dreams and ideals, to sell wholemeal bread or Levi jeans; or by the rise of the unapologetic yuppie, desiring *things* in a supermarket society. Ideas are attractively packaged, them quickly stamped as out-of-date; books are products which, like any other product, may soon be purchase-taxed. The 1980s may well be tagged by history as the decade of consumerism.

A revolution has been taking place within publishing. What has happened in the world of books could be used by conservatives in Britain or the United States as an example of democratic capitalism at its most efficient and advantageous to the consumer. It could also be used, by all those who dislike the present political climate, as an example of the spiritual and cultural vacuum created by materialistic values. It is certainly true that the publishing industry has swiftly turned itself into a well-run, modernised and profit-making business that has left behind the benevolence and elitism of traditional publishing for a more commercial, hard-nosed and populist attitude. But it is also true that many small and independent companies, traditionally the first to promote and encourage ambitious, experimental and radical literature, have been swallowed up in the takeover and merger mania of the last few years; and that the gulf between rich and poor authors has dramatically widened. It is a brutal reminder of the spirit of the age that we regard books as products or 'units'.

There is more money around in the publishing world than ever before – but there is also less sense of cultural commitment. There is certainly greater efficiency in the publishing business – but less sense of dedication to literature. The takeover and merger wave that rocked publishing houses and brought the vast anonymity of conglomerates to their cosy networks; the sudden and fickle interest of the City in the book business; the wild advances suddenly paid out to a few authors; the increasing gulf between those wealthy writers and the others; the new instability of jobs felt by both editors and writers; the hype of publicity – all testify to a moment of change in the world of books that has profoundly affected editor, writer and reader.

At the 1987 Frankfurt Book Fair Günter Grass spoke of the takeover and merger manias, 'the appetite for buying up and gobbling up' and the 'fear of being bought and gobbled up', as the 'spiritual tokens of capitalism'. But his carnivorous metaphor fails to swallow the fact that more money than ever is being spent on a previously underfunded publishing industry; more books, and more 'serious' books, than ever are being bought by the reading public. To denounce the 'spiritual tokens' of capitalism while ignoring its practical advantages is to succumb to the stale gestures of a reflex socialism. The left's and feminism's discomfort with profit in connection with the arts, or with the lucrative business of packaging, marketing and selling creativity, has to be resolved. For the uncomfortable paradox of the publishing tale is that some houses have been rescued by the new internationalism of the book world, and that some writers have 'never had it so good'. It is necessary to look behind the immediate advantages and disadvantages of the publishing revolution to ask what it really means, in the long run, to the kinds of books that are being published, and being written.

Writing in the marketplace

On the shelves of the library or bookshop, the familiar imprints with their distinctive spines are still there. They present a solid and reassuring world of print. The pages of *The Financial Times* or *The Bookseller*, the anxieties of editors as they see their 'safe' careers wobble, the paranoia that lurks in publishing houses fed by rumours that another Goliath is looking for another David, the bemusement of writers who find that in the course of writing one book their publishing house can change hands two or three times, all tell a more action-filled story. From the ouside, it looks as though there is a contagious insanity raging round the world of books. From being a discreet, moderate and relatively private occupation, it is suddenly the Big Time for publishing. It is now an international, multi-million, hi-tech business – and seems to have very little to do with books or their writers. It is difficult to avoid Günter Grass's metaphor of greed (houses being 'bought up and gobbled') or the fear of a collective indigestion where books are pulped, uncommercial writers or whole lists spat out, as financial titans scrap over the last big prizes. There are times when all the buying and selling resembles an expensive game of pass the parcel: no sooner are the spoils grasped than the music starts again.

Between 1982 and 1987 *The Bookseller*, in what it admits to be a 'by no means comprehensive' and immediately out-of-date survey of British publishing, listed more than forty publishing houses making over one hundred major purchases. Some of the changes would be a diagram-drawer's nightmare: Associated Book Publishers buys A.H. & A.W. Reed, Routledge & Kegan Paul (including Pandora) and Croom Helm; ABP is bought by Thomsons, it sells to other conglomerates both Methuen General and Pandora; Bertelsmann buys Doubleday. Chatto, Bodley

Head & Cape buys Virago; Random House buys them; Virago buys out. Century buys Hutchinson, Macmillan buys Sidgwick & Jackson. Octopus – out-tentacling almost everybody else – buys Brimax Books, the Heinemann group, Hamlyn Publishing, a third of Pan, and Mitchell Beazley; Octopus is then bought by Reed International. Penguin buys Thomson Books, which include Michael Joseph and Hamish Hamilton as well as Sphere; Weidenfeld buys Dent.

It is a saga that becomes an epic when you realise the volume of money involved in all the transactions. Associated Book Publishers, with its annual turnover of £85 million, was bought by the massive conglomerate International Thomson Organisation, for whom publishing is just another small arrow in its quiver, for an astonishing £210 million. One month ABP shares were quietly trading in a bull market at 273 pence, three weeks later the company was acquired at 730 pence a share: its market value trebled in twenty-one days. Even allowing for the fact that publishing profits are almost impossible to forecast – and so there will always be big latitudes in prospective bids – this is surely a case of the 'mad bidder'. Except that Thomsons was only a few pence ahead of Gulf & Western and of Pearson.

It is as if, rather, there has been a contagious financial interest in publishing that is both sudden and fickle. London literary agent Anne McDermid thinks that books are the City's 'new toy, new game' with which, because publishing profits are very small in comparison with others, they will rapidly grow bored and discard, moving on to 'cattle or wheat or oil or beans'. The large financial companies or the mass-communication tycoons are not investing in literature but in potential profit; few have very much corporate interest in the future of literature or in its intellectual value. Even those who have clearly done very well out of the takeover trend are anxious about its long-term effects. Graham C. Greene of Cape, who was unwillingly catapulted into the limelight when his uncle, *the* Graham Greene, denounced him in a letter to *The Times*, personally made a large amount of money when his company was sold to Random House. Graham Greene senior subsequently left the group to be published by fellow-

18

exile, the distinguished Max Reinhardt – who set up a small publishing house from his own house in order to bring out Greene's latest novel. Max Reinhardt, when asked whether Graham C. Greene was a 'broken man', replied that if so, he was a 'rich broken man'. Graham C. Greene of Cape admitted that it was a relief to be bought up by the 'good guy' whose 'civilised behaviour' seems to safeguard the literary reputation of Cape – but he also recognised that their purchaser could just as well have been a tycoon with his eye on the profit margin alone, and his mind on the possibility of an accelerated turnover.

Some editors articulate an almost metaphysical disgust at the acquisition boom. New York literary agent Frances Goldin uses it as an example of an age of consumer decadence, in which 'anything is buyable; you can buy people, you can buy companies; publishing has become a commodity and it no longer matters about books' quality'. Others have a more pragmatic and ambivalent approach. It is clear, however, that publishing is in an unprotected and fragile phase. The marketplace, whether it favours or excludes, is ruthless and undiscriminating, and while there are some 'good guys' there are also villains. It is naive to expect a tycoon like Rupert Murdoch, who now owns Collins in the United Kingdom and Doubleday in the United States, or Robert Maxwell, who owns Pergamon Press, carefully to maintain the balance between quality and value. And naive to think that a massive conglomerate like Gulf & Western will have writers' long-term literary futures as a priority.

There is now little sense of cultural philanthropy, which, for all its elitism and paternalism, was at least driven by a moral and cultural impetus rather than a simply materialistic one. And once the publishing industry is opened up to the profit-and-loss and quick turnover world of the large conglomerates, then the possibilities for cultural erasure are significantly increased. Publishers' jobs and authors' books are vulnerable to the accountant's pen. A small independent press may be absorbed into a bigger one which in its turn is swallowed up by an international company; a whole series may be struck off (as in fact happened with the Heinemann African series) because it fails to make a large enough profit margin; poetry may be deemed unworth-while; the feminist books from a mainstram house may start to lose sales and be dropped. Smaller and more radical presses were designed to nurture whole categories of literature until they were strong enough to survive in the mainstream. Now they may be lopped off or not even conceived. In their place the conglomer-ates may start to concentrate upon those products that do not need troublesome and expensive low-volume authors: high-fibre diet books or almanacs and diaries, microwave cookery manuals or glossy coffee table books to complement furnishings.

And among the army of sales reps, publishers, publicists and designers, the actual writers often feel that they are, or are in danger of becoming, the 'producers' of the 'product' that is to be fed into the impressive machinery of publishing. Whereas publishers weigh advantage against disadvantage, balance com-mercial and literary considerations, deal with the accounts and with the writer, and juggle the humanitarian values of literature and the need to make money in a fiercely competitive market-place, the writers increasingly feel like an alienated workforce; the cottage industrialists or piece workers of publishing – neg-lected or invisible, usually badly paid.

Feminist and independent houses: on the fringe with their foot in the centre

Independent and smaller publishers – an increasingly rare phenomenon in the multinationalism of books – can appear as havens of quality, organisations that thrive without being hurled into the stock exchange, that nurture their authors and counter the crasser instincts of their larger competitors Independent, fringe and feminist presses have a tradition of providing space and choice for exciting literature – the old and revered houses of Gollancz and Deutsch; the morally committed and culturally challenging feminist presses like The Women's Press, Pandora, Virago, Sheba or Onlywomen; the struggling, understaffed houses like John Calder or Journeyman Press; the new and thriving Bloomsbury; all become the cultural heroes of the

United Kingdom. In North America tiny presses counter the geographical elitism of New York, while companies such as W.W. Norton (the employee-owned, author- and editor-centred company) successfully compete with the giants on Fifth Avenue.

But it is an error to set up the small and fringe presses as stereotypic models of literary independence, offering space and choice and moral commitment, or to assume that small is inevitably beautiful and big necessarily bad. The recent fortunes of two feminist presses, Virago and The Women's Press, and one mainstream and newly launched one, Bloomsbury, are examples of how the takeover trend can both protect and threaten editorial independence.

Bloomsbury was set up as a direct response to the merger wave. Like Ursula Owen of Virago, its founder Liz Calder has a strictly pragmatic approach to the changes within the publishing world and does not regard the new boom as 'a good or bad thing'. But while she pointed out that general trade publishing is precarious, and there are some cases where a takeover can save a house from collapse, she still considers independent presses the most successful: 'By successful I don't mean successful financially; I mean they produce good books.' Bloomsbury raised over £2 million from the City and launched itself on a glamorous party, an impressive list, books that are designed to make you want them on your shelves – and the promise that it would distinguish itself by an intimate relationship with its authors. The Authors' Trust – a scheme whereby each Bloomsbury author holds shares in the company – and the emphasis on the writer's involvement in the progress of the book through its whole publishing process are Bloomsbury's response to the takeover trend.

But while the Authors' Trust signals a rejection of the hierarchical traditions of publishing, and while the promise of authorial involvement has a potent appeal in an age where publishing houses seem to be hurtling towards large-scale anonymity, Bloomsbury has not in fact radically distinguished itself from its competitors. It has been unapologetically mainstream in its style and content – glossy packaging, effective hype,

21

literary and popular novels jostling together, a spread of subjects from the Falklands War and the life of Pasolini to knitting designs and Elvis Presley. It has spent huge amounts of money on selected authors. It has been conservative in its choice of books, and its attitudes to publishing and selling, while highly professional, have not been so different from those of its competitors. And while it countered the merger boom and anonymous big time of the book business, yet it has depended upon the climate of acquisition and fickle City interest for its capital. The birth of Bloombury demonstrates an enduring paradox of the consumerist climate. It rejected and embraced the predominant spirit of consumerism – and could never have been born without it.

Virago has experienced both independence and ownership. Launched in 1973, it was an instant success. It redeemed classics by women from oblivion, brought readers to feminist fiction who previously had shied away. Its distinctive green bindings took up more and more space in bookshops and then large chains, and its innovative introduction of the trade paperback heralded a new era in paperback publishing. Instant success held its dangers – Virago was in the delicate position of being on the radical and campaigning edge of literature while also being mainstream. And, like most feminist presses, the late 1980s have been difficult for it. It has had to reduce the print-runs of most of its books, from an average of 6,000 to 7,000 to an average of 5,000 to 6,000. Virago merged with the Cape, Chatto & Bodley Head group because, as editor and director Ursula Owen put it, 'at that time we needed to stabilise'. Being part of a bigger group did mean better distribution, a larger and better repping service and improved administration. Sales were boosted, especially overseas. But there was a price to pay. When the whole group went into financial decline, Virago, with its reputation of being 'the goose that lays the golden egg', also suffered with it. Moreover, Ursula Owen recognises that although editorial independence was maintained, Virago books were no longer under the total control of Virago Press. When in 1987 the group was acquired by Random House, Virago bought itself out. After all those rapid changes, Ursula Owen speaks with measured approval both of their experience as part of a group, and of their return to independence. Independence is not intrinsically a better state; independent companies are usually more vulnerable than their rivals who are protected by the umbrella of a larger company. When the cash flow ceases to flow, it is difficult to be flexible and often foolhardy to be ambitious.

The Women's Press is a small feminist house that suddenly found itself with a bestseller. When *The Color Purple* won the Pulitzer Prize for Fiction in April 1983 it had had barely a review in this country; on its award it received some ecstatic responses from the alternative press but bemused or withering attention from the nationals (an example of what Ros de Lanerolle called 'the dead hand of Britain's – England's – critical tradition which couldn't recognise a work of genius when one was thrust under its collective nose'). Nicholas Shrimpton in *The Sunday Times* found it 'drearily predictable'. *The Color Purple* thrived on word-of-mouth praise and was already The Women's Press's best-selling novel before the news broke that it was to be made into a film – what is more, a *Spielberg* film. Ros de Lanerolle learnt, through the razzmatazz and slog that led up to the film's release that 'in terms of sheer logistics, a bestseller is a mixed blessing for a small publisher, and we are conscious of having negotiated a number of rocks that might have wrecked us'. The strain on cash flow, the extra energy needed from hard-working sales, design and publicity staff, the unprecedented advertising programme, endangered both the bank balance and the other authors who are not Pulitzer Prize, Spielberg-famed novelists. And Ros de Lanerolle conceded that *The Color Purple*, while making The Women's Press more confident, more able to take risks, also pushed the press 'into a rate of development we never planned'. But The Women's Press had a safety net – it is part of the Namara Group and therefore has access to money or an overdraft which would not otherwise have been available. It would have been difficult, perhaps even impossible, for The Women's Press to survive its success had it not been part of a larger group.

In 1988 Virago celebrated its fifteenth birthday, and The Women's Press its tenth. Both presses are now part of the literary establishment in a way that would have seemed impossible in the 1970s – and in some ways both are victims of their own success. Struggling to keep a firm position in the swiftly changing marketplace of books, they are both locked into identities that are begining to feel slightly out-of-date. Virago still brings out its famous reprints, but while those were revelations in the late 1970s, gobbled up by thousands of women readers, in the late 1980s, they tend to be mediocre examples of dead women's writing, many of which should have stayed out of print. And while The Women's Press continues to publish many third-world writers, it is now too dominated by its political line and ideological commitments, so that its list has a predictable, slightly worthy flavour. In both cases, the need to consolidate past success and strengthen the identities forged in the 1970s and early 1980s has led to an over-production of novels that often lack literary merit. In the two oldest and most established feminist houses in Britain, little new is happening.

Pandora, which has struggled in the first years of its life to create a distinct identity, has had to plan clearly and explicitly a new direction to take it into the 1990s. Conceived by Philippa Brewster in 1981, and launched in 1983, it was originally part of Routledge & Kegan Paul, where Philippa Brewster was an editor in charge of a cross-disciplinary academic list. She perceived a gap in feminist publishing – where Virago concentrated on reprints, and The Women's Press imported many of their novels, there was no press publishing general feminist non-fiction trade paperbacks. Philippa Brewster admitted to making many mistakes in Pandora's first years, which affected their list – they had no clear idea of a readership, and brought out a 'mishmash' of books, each of which was targetting a different audience. Even the introduction of fiction was done in a sporadic and responsive way: two excellent manuscripts – Jeanette Winterson's Whitbread Prize-winning *Oranges Are Not The Only Fruit* and Andrea Freud Lowenstein's *This Place* – simply landed on her desk.

External circumstances have forced Pandora to reconsider its identity and development. New management at Routledge & Kegan Paul was followed by the merger with Associated Book Publishers; ABP was then taken over by International Thomson and in 1987 Pandora was purchased by Unwin Hyman. Changes have meant wholesale rethinking. In the past Pandora, lacking resources and back-up, had to rely upon reprints. Now, with expertise and money behind them, the emphasis is firmly upon commissioning new material. The fiction list, which in the past has been unplanned and without its own distinctive character, will under Kate Figes apparently take on a clear identity: 'We want contemporary, exciting, international and provocative novels; we think of ourselves as a Woman's Picador.' Kate Figes intends to take risks with fiction (an example of which is *Sweet Death* by the French author Claude Tardat – a compelling and repellent description of one woman's suicide by sugar) and to publish novels that 'create imaginary worlds' rather than reproduce the familiar feminist confessional so prolific in the last decade.

Pandora's plans for its future break with the traditional commitment of the women's presses to books *about* feminism – 'we want books influenced *by* feminism' – question the narrow definition of feminism and of feminist publishing.

Advances and the Emperor's new clothes

The effect of the takover and merger boom and the cultural climate of the 1980s upon publishing houses is contradictory and fraught with discomforting paradoxes. So, too, is the effect upon individual writers. Many presses are suffering from what Gill Davies of Tavistock, the academic press now merged into Routledge, calls 'the nightmare scenario' of 'shrinkage and shrinkage and shrinkage and overheads going higher and higher and higher', in which the person in the front line of subsequent cutbacks is often the writer. But at the same time there are some writers who have 'never had it so good'. Nowhere is the double-edged effect of the takeover wave more evident than in the world of advances. Some writers are wealthier than ever before, others poorer, usually in relative, but sometimes in actual, terms. In a neat reflection of British life, the gulf between them is growing wider and more divisive.

An advance used to be just that: money advanced against subsequent royalties that an author would earn. For most writers it is still a modest sum based on cautious predictions of a book's sale. Some advances can be as little as £150; more often they are in the small thousands. Frequently they are the only money an author will see; almost always they are the only substantial amount a book earns, followed by dribbles and trickles from its life in the marketplace. But 'advance' has taken on another meaning for a few writers: that of transfer fee, prestige money – publishing madness. Since publishing became multinational, advances for the hunted few have escalated into fantasy land, separating the majority of writers from the money-spinning stars. Suddenly the leviathans of print have been able to afford giant sums of money. The takeover war is continued in the scrabble for individual contracts. (Chatto's acquision of Michael Holroyd's biography of George Bernard Shaw for £625,000 would not, for example, have been possible without the Random House purchase of their group.) The wilder advances are usually paid by a publisher in order to beat off the opposition and keep an author, in order to take over an author from her previous house, or in order to advertise an imprint. Graham C. Greene frankly admitted that Chatto's acquisition of Holroyd's biography was worth the money for the publicity and the boost to Chatto's literary reputation as well as for the book itself.

It is a mad world, far removed from the traditionally genteel semi-poverty with which most writers are associated. Nothing speaks more clearly of the changes in publishing than the rows of noughts that now push some writers into the wealth bracket. Catherine Cookson left Heinemann for Bantam for a £4 million, ten-book deal; the paperback rights for Sue Miller's first novel, *The Good Mother*, were sold by Gollancz to Pan for £100,000; the UK rights for Marilyn French's *Her Mother's Daughter* were sold to Heinemann for £275,000; the US rights for Elizabeth Adler's *Peach* were sold to Dell/Delacorte for $300,000; Susan

Howatch left Hamish Hamilton for Collins for £800,000; Fay Weldon left Hodder & Stoughton for Collins for £450,000; the UK rights for Shirley Conran's *Savages* were £850,000; Salman Rushdie earned a £1.5 million advance for *The Satanic Verses*.

But there is something surreal going on. Many of these advances simply do not make straightforward financial sense. Fay Weldon has transferred to Collins, but *Leader of the Band* will have to sell approximately twice as many copies, both in hardback and paperback, than she has ever sold before, in order to earn its advance of £450,000. And there is a Catch 22 in operation, whereby publishers make sure that those books bought for massive, even absurd, sums will still be profitable. It is a form of artificially induced success. In 1987 Sally Beauman's *Destiny* was published; a tale of sex, wealth, power, passions and intrigue, it had all the ingredients of a blockbusting bestseller. But so do many other fat and juicy novels. *Destiny* was bought in the UK for £385,000 and in the States for a staggering $1,015,000. It was in many ways an arbitrary choice. Publishers needed a blockbusting lead title; several mainstream houses got involved in the auction and started outbidding each other in manic competition – and suddenly she found herself a wealthy woman, a figure who could have walked out of the pages of her potboiler.

Now *Destiny* will probably earn its advance – indeed, the advance acts as a self-fulfilling prophecy. The novel had massive publicity well before it was published because of the money paid for it; the publishers put large sums into advertising it. It was widely (and badly) reviewed on publication, and prominently displayed in every large bookshop in Britain. But for every *Destiny* there are dozens of similar novels that earn nothing like Sally Beauman's advance – and hundreds of 'serious' books that seem to live in an entirely different element. Sally Beauman defends *Destiny* against the charges of gratuitous sex (she thinks the attacks would be muted if she was not English, and not there at all if she was a man), the claims that sex occurs every ten pages (she's counted, and it is approximately every sixteen), and the gleeful criticism of her writing. She is sanguine – well, who wouldn't be after earning more than a million dollars? – about the reviews ('I don't see any point in being deeply upset about being bludgeoned with a big stick'). *Destiny* was never meant to be 'literary'.

> One interviewer said, 'Why didn't you write a serious
> book, why didn't you set out to win the Booker Prize?' I
> think that is a most extraordinary question. I felt I might
> be capable of writing a popular book but if I had felt
> capable of writing a wonderful P.D. James or Ruth
> Rendell type of book, then I would have written that.

But she concedes that it is 'lamentable that good books are produced which are bought for peanuts and read by hardly anyone'.

In the USA, where books have a much larger potential audience and therefore publishing is a bigger business than in the UK, it is not so unusual to pay over $1 million for a book. But American editors are equally bemused and dismayed by the amounts now being paid to individual authors, and the effect it has upon author and house. They often come up with specific reasons for the wild expenditure. Anne Godoff of Atlantic Press blames the 'loss-leader mentality' ('the notion of deliberately paying too much money in order to take that person's name out to lunch with you') which makes an editor 'jaded and cynical'. Kathy Anderson of Simon & Schuster focuses upon an editor's need to establish his or her reputation swiftly ('you have a lot of editors moving around now, and they want to establish their immediate identity so they buy writers and they write cheques and it doesn't really matter what they spend'). However, several other New York editors are frank about their bewilderment and shocked by the collective advance fever. They cite examples of first-time novelists whose mildly promising books are bought for sums of money that make one ask: 'What is all the excitement about?'

For behind the specific reasons of individual editors, behind the advance fever and the excitement of the takeover trends, is the real and justified fear that we are seeing a model example of the Emperor's new clothes – a complicated game of deception and self-deception is disrupting the flawed but discriminating meritocracy of the publishing world.

Advance-wildness produces a self-generating excitement, a world of big money, nail-biting deals, shadiness and glamour; a world far removed from the daily grind of the crowd of authors in their lonely rooms or the majority of editors who are buying books for modest sums and expecting modest print-runs. It is not, however, an entirely sealed-off world – the knock-on effect is felt by all involved in the process, whether it be because one *Destiny* signals a Darwinian world in which a dozen books are condemned to instant oblivion, or because publishing houses are threatened by the predatory environment in which their staple authors are poached.

The perils and paradoxes of feminist presses in the marketplace

Feminist presses are at risk in the present acquisitive climate, and are facing a series of direct threats to the position they have carved out for themselves in the marketplace. They are now more likely to lose authors whose books they first published, whose reputations they nurtured and whose names, once known, are sought by publishers with greater clout and purchasing power. It is an anxiety that lies at the heart of many feminist presses, for they often have an ambiguous relationship with mainstream publishing. Both Ursula Owen of Virago and Ros de Lanerolle of The Women's Press recognised from the beginning that losing authors, and acting as stepping stones to aid them into the mainstream, was an inevitable part of success. As Anne McDermid pointed out, the kind of attention that a writer will receive from a feminist press 'pales into insignificance in comparison with the big money that can come their way from the major commercial houses'.

What feminist and smaller independent presses offer their authors is involvement, commitment, and intimate encouragement. But such advantages are clearly not the prerogative of smaller operations and sometimes the author-publisher relationship can break down under financial strain. Ursula Owen sees an 'unresolvable conflict' in the way that 'ideologically motivated' houses are run. Virago is a feminist publisher that has to run along capitalist lines; the ideological 'cause' is the book, often at the expense of the writer, and even the staff. John Calder provides another example of a small and threatened publishing business that must abuse writers in order to bring out their works. Calder has struggled to promote fine international literature and has brought many authors to Britain (Beckett is the most striking example) – but often he cannot pay them their royalties. If he did, his house would fall and another avenue for writers would cease to exist. The poorer presses can veer towards exploitation and self-exploitation in order to bring out the literature in which they so passionately believe.

And Virago has its own clear example of the ideological difficulties of publishing; a feminist press may not necessarily be the most sympathetic or enabling house for a feminist author. Zoë Fairbairns's best-selling novel, the family saga *Stand We At Last*, was commissioned by Virago. While she recognises that she was 'well and promptly paid', the experience of writing the novel soured her partnership with Virago because (and as she says 'you will have to decide for yourself whether or not I am a reliable narrator') 'they wanted me to write Virago books rather than Zoë Fairbairns books' and 'were specifically applying pressure on me to change the way that I write for commercial purposes'. She is alert to the ironies of a feminist press behaving in an authoritarian fashion, but recognises that Virago was then 'a small struggling business' needing to make money. She uses her cautionary tale, rather, as a denunciation of 'the wonderful myth among feminists that these things don't happen in the feminist presses, they only happen with the big baddie'. She points out that it is very often the bigger presses, without ideological commitments or even a commitment to literature of quality, which can afford to treat their writers well. It is a bitter irony that ideologically committed presses producing radical texts are often forced to compromise more than their commercially motivated rivals.

In Britain the feminist presses are perilously positioned. They are on the fringe with their foot in the centre; ideologically committed in a capitalist marketplace. The fact that writers are lured away by bigger money is a reminder of the intrinsic vulnerability of feminist houses: ever since they were born they have had to contend with big presses who take up and appropriate what they have made commercially viable. Women readers have for a long time been the main buyers and borrowers of books – even if much of their buying and borrowing has been done on behalf of men. They were hungry for the kind of books that Virago, The Women's Press, Pandora, Sheba and Only-women produced, treating women not as appendages in a male world but as central. The success of the feminist books, coinciding with the growth in feminist awareness in the 1970s, alerted mainstream houses to a 'gap' in the market. Now there are very few big publishers that do not have a women's list. As Ros de Lanerolle comments, there was a time when you could 'call a book feminist and it was bound to sell'.

At first glance, this kind of appropriation appears galling for the feminist presses, but to the advantage of the reader, and in the long run of feminism itself. The process of popularisation and accessibility has long been a goal of feminist writers and editors, who were conscious that feminism traditionally had a middle-class, white and elitist appeal. In the words of Kate Mosse, editor at Century Hutchinson and member of Women in Publishing, it is unjust that bigger companies 'who have done bugger all except listen to their business sense' should grab the spoils from feminist presses. But, she insists, the priority among feminist publishers must be accessibility – to 'spread the word in an almost revolutionary way'.

Beneath the pattern of appropriation of feminist books by mainstream presses, and their welcome increased availability, a threat is discernible that has little to do with the obvious and immediate risk to women's houses. Pandora, The Women's Press, Sheba and Virago have initiated and nurtured whole categories of writing, until they are strong enough to be absorbed by mainstream companies. There the books are unprotected: dips in the profit line, a decline in their short-term popularity, threaten their very existence. Feminist presses keep an eye on a book's profit, but also upon its cultural significance. Even Elspeth Lindner of Methuen, who aspires to providing a 'bridge' between the radical and established presses, recognises that the mediating and tactful nature of her task means that Methuen cannot be 'at the campaigning or radical sharp end of publishing'.

Naturally authors will leave small presses for larger ones – they have to pay their gas bills – but the danger of a one-way flow is that certain types of feminist writing will be lost. The argument that women's presses actually should decline and fall once they have done their job of introducing feminism to the general reading public ignores the fact that only by continually reintroducing feminist works to the mainstream does feminist and radical literature develop. The ways in which major commercial houses can treat their lists suggest the cultural glaciation or erasure that would occur without fringe publishers.

The editor and author: a frail partnership

Editors on both sides of the Atlantic stress 'partnership' between themselves and their writers, defining their role along the lines laid down by Anne Godoff of New York's Atlantic Press: 'the writer's first and best reader, their advocate and their critic'. Writers, however, are not so sure. Their ambivalence often edges into a feeling of bitterness and betrayal. Certainly the partnership, always a tenuous affair, is more fragile than ever before. In the fluctuating world of publishing, where houses are bought up, editors leave houses and authors are lured away with larger advances, it is as if the writers as well as their works have become the product, up for grabs. Writers regret the lost continuity and loyalty, especially women writers who have moved on from (or been moved on from) the feminist presses that first published and encouraged them. But the author/editor relationship has built-in complications: the editor gets a salary and security denied to the writer; necessary professionalism often collides with the very personal and emotional feelings that a writer has towards her words. Above all, the writer, especially at the beginning of her career, is in a weak negotiating position and feels grateful to be published at all. Even today, with the growth of protective agreements by publishers and libraries, writers remain a collection of solitary and scattered individuals, rather than a group with recognised rights of employment.

A confidential survey carried out by the Society of Authors and the Writer's Guild in September 1988 emphasised how unsatisfied many authors were with their publishers. Authors were asked to rate their publishers, on a point scale of one to five, in sixteen different areas of performance, from adherence to the terms of contract and promptness of payment to the quality and efficiency of promotion and readiness to inform the author. Few of the seventy-five houses for which five or more returns were received scored higher than four; an alarming number scored under 3.5. It may be significant that the top ten in the League Table are all small or comparatively small houses – but so, too, are many of those right at the bottom. Michael Legat, who analysed and reviewed the responses to the questionnaire, emphasised that the biggest problem in author/publisher relationships is 'a failure to communicate'. He also insisted that the responsibility 'must lie squarely with the publisher'.

A widespread dissatisfaction among writers surfaces in such a survey, where confidentiality is guaranteed. Its sources, however, are difficult to eradicate. Publishers too easily dismiss writers' complaints as whingeing, rightly pointing out that they choose their publisher, receive their royalties and are free to leave their editor whenever they choose. But the old reliance of a writer upon her publisher, and the old expectations of mutual loyalty, are not lightly abandoned for a more hard-headed commercial approach.

The solitary writer often needs an ally; she may stick with her press long after she should have left, consumed by a self-abasing and destructive form of gratitude, witheringly expressed by Fay Weldon: 'What! Publish my work? Oh thank you! Exploit me, cheat me, jump on me, unworthy me, anything so long as you publish, oh thank you!' For many writers, even those who are well-established and widely read, are consumed by the fear of *not* being published. Leslie Dick, whose first novel, *Without Falling*, landed wrapped in brown paper on dozens of publishers' desks before being taken up by the newly launched Serpent's Tail, draws a parallel between being unpublished and being unemployed: 'It is all about who is in and who is out.' Once you have been published once, you will be considered seriously; before that, you are not a 'writer'.

Even Emma Tennant, who jauntily calls herself a 'publisher skipper', explains how she skipped against her own will. Her first two novels were published by Cape, who then rejected her third, *Hotel du Dream*, which was accepted by Kevin Crossley-Holland of Gollancz. That novel did rather well, and she returned, with editor Liz Calder, to Cape, which then brought out *Wild Nights*. Three books later, and *Women Beware Woman* was published. But to her shock and horror Emma Tennant then read a review identifying the real characters from whom her fictional figures had evolved. On investigation it turned out that the novel's libel notes had been sent out with the review copies. It was every writer's nightmare, and she left Cape for Faber & Faber, where she has since remained. Emma Tennant stressed that she would have preferred to remain with a single editor and publishing house. Loyalty and the desire for stability are potent emotions, for without them writers become even more solitary figures in a publishing landscape which can often seem hostile. Their 'advocate and critic' becomes the agent, who mediates between 'partners'.

Maggie Gee's experience has taught her that a writer's vulnerability leaves her open to abuse, for 'writers can be flattered and publishers are very long on flattery – you know, hideously embarrassing letters about how wonderful your novel is, followed by an offer of £500 (I got £500 for my first novel).' Like any other form of unemployment, you cannot get published until you have been published, and 'you will do almost anything to get that book born'. She has her own naive confession:

> I chose Faber & Faber out of snobbery. Faber: they
> published Auden and they published Eliot; it was a dream

they should ever publish me. After *Dying in Other Words*
[published by Harvester] came out I had this letter from
Robert McCrum of Faber, saying I was the most exciting
thing since blah blah, and they would love to see my
next novel. I literally framed it. I was so excited that I
didn't even answer.

Maggie Gee suffers from the common complaint of writer's
embarrassment when dealing with money matters.

I find dealing with money hard. It is ridiculous – I mean,
with the bit of reviewing and journalism I do, before I say
'yes' or 'no' I know that I should ask 'How much?' But I
usually say 'How much?' after I've said yes – and then I
say it in a rather embarrassed way: it is not important to
me, you know, but could you just mention the price.
Actually I need to know – £70: maybe I could do it; £100:
great; £35: there's no way it is worth my time when I
haven't got very much time. But there is still this very
shadowy area where we are supposed to love writing so
much that we want to do it for free.

Like every other author, Sara Maitland has her gripes,
although her relationship with editors has usually been good. She
says that 'almost every person I know both loves and loathes their
publishers', and she has a 'grudge' about the way publishing
houses 'make quite arbitrary decisions about which books they
will push and which books they won't – and that radically affects
sales and radically affects income. That makes me angry –
especially when I think I could have done a better job myself.'
She makes the inevitable comparison between the comfortable
or wealthy world in which her book is published, and her private
world in which it is written.

I'm always suspicious of publishers who take you out to
lunch and then say they can't afford to pay you any more
– there's a bit in me which thinks, 'At least give me the

£60 this lunch has cost and let me go home and do some work.' And the same goes for some publication parties – there's a bit in me that looks around at the amount of drink that is being consumed and thinks that this is not going to make any more out of the book, nobody is going to have a particularly good time just because we gave this party – why not stuff it and send me the cash. Of course, it is possible to do it right, as they did for *Virgin Territory*. But it is a particularly difficult relationship because of the economic differences.

Essentially, the people in the publishing house are going to get their salary whatever happens. They will be paid at the end of the month regardless of the product. And they get a pension at the end of it. And because that is the case little things become galling. It is jolly hard, when writing to the accounts people to remind them they are late with payment, not to feel that if they themselves were paid on commission they would make sure it wasn't two minutes late. And they wouldn't suggest holding back 20 per cent of their income each quarter to recover the returns – that is outrageous.

Even editors, insistent that they have their authors' best interests at heart, recognise that the structure of publishing makes it a relationship that is fraught with potential conflict. Yes, it is in their interests that writers are well treated and as well paid as possible; yes, it is true that in the long term an editor's career depends upon the fortunes of her books, just as a writer's does. But as Liz Calder of Bloomsbury points out, the 'uneasy' relationship between editor and author might well be 'endemic'. The publisher 'can never do enough for the author'. The book is 'the be all and end all' for its writer and the editor can never satisfy her anxious expectations.

The isolated insecurity of writing is usually intensified when the writer is a woman. For many men, the solitariness of writing is ameliorated by the presence of a wife or partner, who will wash his clothes and care for his children, feed and cosset him – ending up, more often than not, as the 'without whom' in the dedication. Few women have the emotional and practical support that a wife brings. They either live independently, or they *are* the wife, writing in the hours between the cooking and clothing and washing and childcare. Some are lucky enough to have husbands who expect to share domestic burdens – but almost none have husbands who will act, even in times of stress and approaching deadlines, as 'wives'. Inevitably, the act of writing is often squeezed into corners of a domestic day. Feminism has tended to concentrate on women working outside the home, so that those who remain within the private domestic sphere can easily drop through its formal organisations and informal networks. The profound isolation that a woman can suffer when writing makes her relationship with her editor more important than ever – and more vulnerable to impossible demands.

The demands and expectations are sharpened and made more personal when women writers are being published by a *feminist* press. Gill Davies recognises that writing, especially for some women, is 'a very lonely and emotionally traumatic experience', but as a professional she dislikes the way that 'a lot of women coming to an editor with a feminist list expect another kind of relationship beyond the professional one. If you let them down – and of course we do let them down sometimes – there is a feeling of personal betrayal.' There was a time when Gill Davies considered turning Tavistock into a specifically feminist house.

> I didn't because I don't want to be an icon; I don't want
> to be trying to hold a set of political positions which I
> can't necessarily fulfil; I don't want the author
> relationship to be so total that the professional
> arrangements go to one side. You can't do your
> professional best if you allow yourself to get too close.

However good the editor, the author will often feel painfully isolated. Working in solitude, she needs affirmation at the very time that she cannot receive it, and is forever unsure that she will write again. She is surrounded by the paraphernalia of book production – the agent, editor, designer, sales force – but she is not of it. She does not even belong to the machinery of publishing, but delivers her manuscript into its jaws.

t w o

THE STAR SYSTEM

<hr>

Publicity: the writers' Catch 22

Feminists have attacked the feminism of the late 1980s for subsuming its real meaning into style. Statements of assertion, independence and individuality are made through dress and appearance: women taking an exotic pleasure in their street-wise, radical-chic appearance; women wearing short, tight skirts, outrageous dresses, faces framed by wild ear-rings whose decorations take the place of make-up. The days when women deliberately dressed down to emphasise that they should not be judged by their carefully prepared looks – those over-parodied dungarees and cropped haircuts – have been replaced by deliberate and often mocking self-presentation. The women in the street with their dramatic clothes and unmade-up faces are not presenting onlookers with the signs of their availability so much as taking pleasure in themselves. But some older feminists have seen in their carefully cultivated images an implicit rejection of the solidarity and sisterhood of early feminism in favour of the more individually assertive and consumer-conscious feminism of the 1980s.

And while some of these complaints can be unattractively puritanical and authoritarian, applying a heavy-handed morality to trivia, the underlying anxiety can seem justified. There are times when feminism dissipates into an *image* of feminism. The anxiety also has its roots in a traditional unease with style, attractive packaging, glossiness – as if an idea or movement will atrophy beneath the image, as if eye-catching designs are there to conceal a lack of substance, as if efficient packaging reduces a philosophy to a commodity. But in the world of books – as in the world of politics – the creation of an image has become an essential part of the business. Book design, promotion and publicity no longer simply announce a book; they *sell* it. Most feminist presses have recently been as effective as their main-stream competitors at carefully creating the image that will sell the book.

The whiff of unease should remain. Books as products, writers as marketable personalities, editors as managers of a commodity, mean that a justifiable comparison is often made between publishing houses and supermarkets, imprints and brand names, novels and consumer items that you can pick off the shelves. Of course, such a comparison applies only to books published by bigger presses and well distributed and marketed; those produced by smaller presses are not so lucky. But from the point that most books leave the publishing house, they are subject to the massive industry of distribution and publicity hype. Sometimes this is well-organised presentation of a worthy book; sometimes it is a case of the Emperor's new clothes.

Editors are aware of the new importance of image and pub-licity. Nowadays most books need heavy promotion in order to sell – as Kate Mosse in London puts it, 'you've got to start treating books as a commodity like everything else', or as Mary Cunnane in New York regretfully admits, editors must start to behave like 'product managers, like manufacturers of the latest kind of orange juice'. This is precisely the attitude that New York literary agent Frances Goldin rejects, for she believes that 'practi-cally any book can be sold through publicity'. What you get is a 'hyped market', in which trend-conscious writers produce trendy books, debilitating the general state of literature.

The great noise of publicity and hype disguises the fact that many novels are left to silence and slow death. Frances Goldin believes that 'more than half the books which are published would be better off not published', not because of their quality but because of the treatment they receive. Mid-list books can be almost unannounced or unsupported; they are brought out and after the short season they are dead. An author might spend five years on her book to give it three months of half-life, and no money after the advance. London literary agent Anne McDermid pointed out that while literary and new writers *are* getting published, yet 'the gap between the treatment of a Fay Weldon and that of an author who may turn out to be a Fay Weldon is unimaginable'.

There are exceptions – but most books live or die by marketing or its absence. Sally Beauman herself admits that her success took her by surprise: her novel travelled the red carpet way to airport bookshop display and mass sales. With its large advance, its subsequent guaranteed review coverage and its massive publicity campaign, it could scarcely fail to rocket to number one of the bestseller list. Does this then mean that as long as a blockbuster fulfils certain expectations (and, steamy and long and fast-paced, *Destiny* does), then it hardly matters what that novel is like? Sally Beauman is vehement in her 'no'.

> First of all, the idea that you could do that – take a pig's ear and turn it into a silk purse – that seems to me very patronising towards readers. It assumes they have no judgment whatsoever. Secondly, there have been numerous examples of publishers spending a great deal on a book, and publicising it at vast expense, and of that book then disappearing without trace. There have also been examples of books which received, initially, very little publicity, even mediocre reviews, and which then went on to sell millions of copies. John Fowles's *The Magus* is one example; *Watership Down* is another. They sold on word of mouth, and I think that is what ultimately sells any book.
>
> I think people tend to underestimate popular bestsellers – particularly critics who read very little popular fiction. They read maybe one Jackie Collins, and sniff at it; what

they don't read is the hundreds of also-rans – the books which tried to emulate Collins or Krantz or Sheldon, and failed. If you do read some of those, you see a distinction. Collins, Krantz, Sheldon – Stephen King – you may not like what they do but it is possible to see that they do it better than their imitators. And that is why they sell – not because of their marketing.

Sally Beauman's defence is that marketing helps, but that a book must be good of its kind in order to sell. But, as Maureen Duffy points out, 'Advertising sells everything else – why not books?' There can be little doubt that effective hard-nosed hype can manufacture a market which formula novels then feed. And it is optimistic to believe that badly written books will not succeed, however much money has been spent on them: Jeffrey Archer's novels are wooden and tedious, but the marketing of his personality and product has been so well-managed and forceful that that scarcely seems to matter. If it is patronising to suggest that readers can be manipulated by publicity, it is equally patronising to suppose them wilfully fixed upon blockbusting novels of little merit. Experience has demonstrated that readers who traditionally turn to formula fiction can be led towards more individual novels by publicity. Every television dramatisation of a classic novel boosts that novel's sales dramatically. When *The Color Purple* was made into a film, people who would never previously have opened a feminist novel by a black American bought it. Neither does Sally Beauman here consider the stark photo-negative of her argument: that without promotion a book, however good it may be, will rarely reach its potential readers. Lack of advertising condemns it to oblivion.

Penelope Fitzgerald, who believes that 'on the whole publishers are able to manufacture bestsellers', points out that careful accounting is the literary author's Catch 22: 'they calculate how much they think you can sell and then they allocate a certain percentage of that to publicity. So if they don't think you are going to sell very well they don't give you any publicity and sure enough you don't sell very well. You are caught in a trap.'

It is a trap that most authors have experienced some time during their career. Sara Maitland points to the treatment of her *Arky Types*, co-written with Michelene Wandor. It is an epistolary joke, an eccentric and bubbly exploration of writers' pre-occupations interwoven with tall tales – but it fell flat on publication. 'I honestly believe that it could have been so much better marketed. With a bit more intelligence and oomph, Methuen could have sold it as the alternative cult book for Christmas.'

Again, the smallness of some independent and feminist presses seems to the authors' advantage. At Pandora or Sheba or Only-women, at John Calder or Journeyman or The Women's Press, they might not have vast amounts of money to lift a book to stardom. But they do have the dedication to individual books that prevents them from disappearing into the bog of the so-called 'mid-list'. A mid-list book, according to Philippa Brewster of Pandora, often simply means that all the publicity a novel will get is a mention in the publisher's catalogue.

Reviews

One of the most important forms of publicity for a book is the review page of newspapers and magazines. But with the enormous and growing number of books published each year (in Britain in 1987 a record of 59,837, up by 3 to 4 per cent on the previous year's record), it is quite common for mid-list and first novels to be greeted by what Canadian novelist Jane Rule ruefully recalls as, 'a resounding silence'.

Reviewing the Reviews, a recent publication by Women in Publishing which considers 'A Woman's Place on the Book Page' (its subtitle), demonstrates that books by women suffer on the review pages of national newspapers and magazines. In spite of the flaws of Women in Publishing's study (it does not properly account for he role of women's magazines and the fact that more men have their books published and therefore more men are bound to be reviewed), it remains a disturbing compilation of facts and figures. For example, *The Times Literary Supplement* gives women about 20 per cent of its reviewing space, *The Guardian* about 18 per cent, *The Daily Telegraph* and *The New Statesman* (unlikely partners) romp home with 27 per cent. *The London Review of Books* gives women a miserable 16 per cent (and 86 per cent of its reviewers are male).

Moreover, feminist presses suffer a further setback: literary editors and reviewers tend to favour hardback books over paperback ones – and of course most feminist presses publish their authors in paperback. Elspeth Lindner of Methuen reveals that they, like other publishing houses, will often bring out a few hundred hardback editions simply 'to generate review coverage'. Barbara Wilson, American author and editor of the feminist Seal Press, expresses her incredulity that

> Virago, The Women's Press, Pandora, etc. publish so many good books yet never do I see them reviewed. And that is really tragic for the literary authors who go with them – I don't actually think it is so bad for the die-hard lesbian feminists; they have a public they reach through the grapevine: nobody else might buy those books but your own small group will. Whereas with literary authors, their books will just die.

Few writers have been so abused by the media as North American Andrea Dworkin. Her feminist diatribes, from *Pornography* to *Intercourse*, and her novel *Ice and Fire* have aroused a strange mixture of fascination and a pronounced tendency to describe her 'repulsive' appearance. It is not surprising that she causes such high feeling. *Intercourse*, for instance, is a peculiarly unpleasant book, a sustained indictment of sexual intercourse which she regards as 'the pure, sterile, formal expression of men's contempt for women'; those women who claim to actually enjoy it have 'capitulated'. Heterosexuality, it seems, is a slavery, a 'self-mutilation'. Men use the penis to deliver death to women who are, 'literally, in their genitals, dirt to the men'. Marguerite Duras, among others, is condemned roundly for being a slavish capitulator to the myth of heterosexual desire; Joan of Arc is one of the few heroines (she actually killed men).

Perhaps it is the onslaught from the media ('reviews to wipe my arse on' as she herself graphically puts it) that has led Andrea Dworkin to believe that it is 'ethically shocking' for a woman to write a damning review of another woman's book – particularly in *The New York Times* – even if it is a bad piece of work. She sees that as part of the war men wage against women, defeating women by a strategy of divide and rule:

> I think that all books should be treated with a whole lot
> of love and respect – and I mean all books, including bad
> books. There are ways of writing about bad books.
> Women in particular should not allow themselves to be
> used as the chicks up front in a war against women.

Andrea Dworkin is unlike most women writers, for she is wholeheartedly dedicated to a gendered conspiracy theory of the world. But there are a great many women who feel that male authors have been given a head start simply because of a climate of unconscious bias.

Anne McDermid considers that

> it is very difficult nowadays for any publisher to express a
> preference for male writers – it's an unfashionable view.
> However there are certain literary editors who, if you ask
> them who they think is interesting at the moment, will
> never mention a woman's name in their list. They think
> men are interested in men, men are writing about what
> they, as men, want to read. They would consider that Fay
> Weldon writes kitchen sink novels – they don't even
> think of her in literary terms.

When Doris Lessing wrote her pseudonymous *The Diaries of Jane Somers*, her experience encapsulated much of what is wrong but inevitable with the ways in which books are noticed and reviewed. She revealed in the preface to the reprinted *Diaries* that she had chosen to write a pseudonymous novel for several reasons. She wanted to be reviewed 'on merit, as a new writer, without the benefit of a "name"; to get free of that cage of associations and labels that every established writer has to learn to live inside'. She wanted to cheer up younger writers, 'who often have such a hard time of it', by demonstrating that the ways in which their novels are treated has little to do with their talent. And she wanted to strike back at critics who, hating the *Canopus* series, had been asking for a return to the realism of *The Golden Notebook*. Not one of these critics recognised Doris Lessing beneath Jane Somers.

Perhaps that is not wholly surprising – Jane Somers, released from a constraining label and 'the dryness, like a conscience, that monitors Doris Lessing whatever she writes', produced a very different novel from *The Golden Notebook*. But her experience of the publishing process as an established/new writer held its insights. Her main publishers in Britain were approached first. Cape turned *The Diary of a Good Neighbour* down flat and Granada refused it on the grounds that it was 'too depressing'. On publication (by Michael Joseph in the United Kingdom and Knopf in the United States) the novel received some 'nice little reviews', had very little publicity since (for obvious reasons) there was no personality to promote, and sold 2,800 copies in America; 1,600 in Britain. Even the second Jane Somers novel, *If the Old Could...*, would have been remaindered and pulped within a few months of its first publication. In short, it was treated as most novels by unestablished writers: with a little patronisation and a good deal of indifference. When Doris Lessing came clean, the *Diaries* were rereviewed – and some critics 'seemed inclined retrospectively to find merit'.

The affair of the *Diaries* did not really demonstrate that critics had been unfair to 'Jane Somers'. Indeed, Lessing readily admits that they are often over-attentive to her as a controversial and respected writer, and their treatment of Jane Somers was simply even-handed, if dispiriting. But it did illustrate that the processes and attitudes to which a new writer submits are mechanical, and usually have very little to do with subject or talent. And it also illustrated how hard it is for writers to break through those processes to grab media attention. They usually manage to do so through some whimsical or clever piece of hype. As Lessing wrote

> in order to sell a book, in order to bring it to attention, you need more than the book, you need the television appearance. Many writers who at the start resisted have thought it over, have understood that this, now, is how the machinery works, and they have decided that if – even if it is not acknowledged – they have become part of the sales department of their publishers, then they will do the job as well as they can.

Of course, as Jane Somers discovered and as Doris Lessing very well knows, the danger of hype is that it can sell what is mediocre, as well as what is talented, that it can market gimmicks as successfully as the 'real' thing. And that that would seem to have very little to do with 'literature'.

Hype and its damage: stars and shooting stars

The machinery of publicity has two large dangers. Because it is both undiscriminating and exclusive it misleads the reading public, pushing some books to bestsellerdom and condemning others to instant oblivion. It can also ruin promising writers: they start to believe the hype, and no longer cast a critical eye upon their work.

The Caribbean novelist Joan Riley makes the refreshingly frank and unusual complaint that her novels have been too well reviewed. She believes that because she is a black writer she has been tokenised and hyped in a way which is momentarily gratifying but actually damaging:

> They hype you and you start to believe the hype and then your writing can get pretty bad. They do that with any black person they feel can compete. *The Unbelonging* is certainly not the greatest of novels: not brilliant, not even

that good. I look at it now and think, gosh, I would restructure the whole thing. As a first novel it was all right – nothing to write home about – but it got this big rave, this big hype. Now I could have done one of two things: I could have believed the hype and gone along with it – oh wonderful me, I'm such a great writer. Or I could have taken it with a cartload of salt and gone back home and tried to do something about my writing. I chose to do the latter – but it is very hard to do that because the hype is so good.

When you get a performing monkey you've got to give it exposure, you see. Most of us are considered performing monkeys – and look, it talks! When you get abnormal exposure what they are actually saying is, 'Gosh, it is actually good and it is written by a black woman.' I remember when I was at university and given black literature to read they'd imply, 'Now what you've got to realise is that they cannot actually aspire to the same standards as real literature but they've got a raw primitiveness about them.' And I always vowed that nobody would ever ever say that I had a raw primitiveness.

You're told you are the greatest thing in the black community. And I think – well, if I'm the greatest thing, my God, what do they think about the black community? Is this the level they think we can aspire to? I'm quite happy to be a minute fish in a huge pond; I don't want to be an artificially enlarged fish in a little bit of tap water. I keep my feet planted firmly on the ground. The ink hadn't even dried on my first book and people were talking about this great writer. I have been really shocked because I couldn't understand this gap between people's perceptions of me and my perception of myself. All I do is go home and write.

Barbara Burford wrote in *The New Statesman* about the way in which, in America, and particularly since Alice Walker's *The*

Color Purple won the Pulitzer Prize, 'black women's writing has been used by so many to convey radical chic that our words, often written directly out of pain and disillusionment, are in danger of being taken *totally* out of context'. She echoes Joan Riley's fears that the media will simply gesture towards an approved few: 'we need a drift of many-hued poppies in the pale wheatfield of British publishing and not the occasional specimen flower, spaced strategically here and there'.

Both Barbara Burford and Joan Riley urge British publishers to take on the divergent voices of British black women rather than rely on the 'ethno-cred-gloss' of publishing American women. Burford rightly points out that in the States the tendency to elevate a few writers creates a Hollywood-type star system.

Authors are taken up as today's flavour by the publisher, the media and then the public. Suddenly rich, famous and courted, they become social stars, guests on chat shows, pundits on the radio; they dance their way across the pages of fashion magazines, sell products for TV commercials. It seems to have very little to do with the literary merit of their work, but is dependent upon whether they have marketable personalities.

Many writers resist the razzmatazz and the white Cadillac whistle-stop tour. Mary Gordon has refused to be 'taken up' by her admiring critics. Mona Simpson, whose first novel *Anywhere But Here* was an overnight success, quietly returned to her writing, aware that 'the first novel is often acclaimed and the second ignored' and that to believe the critics leads to a 'stressful sense of fragility'. Sue Miller, whose *The Good Mother* catapulted her to fame, insists that there was only 'all this fuss' because of the book's coincidental topicality.

But if, as Barbara Wilson claims, Americans love above all the trinity of 'youth, attractiveness and stardom', then an author who can manage to combine three in one is a winner. And it is hard to resist the lure of instant literary success. Someone like Tama Janowitz was the perfect item for her publishers: hardly out of college, articulate and self-confident, attractive and zany, with a book, *Slaves of New York*, that caught the narcissistic,

pulsating and despairing energy of big city life and death, she was taken up into the stratosphere of brief stardom. She appeared, glamorous and controversial, on numerous television programmes in numerous states. Andy Warhol pronounced himself ready to come out of retirement to make a film of her book. The media gave her rave reviews, money flowed towards her. She seemed to epitomise the American Dream – young, previously unheard of, and overnight becoming the darling of the media. But Tama Janowitz's second novel was not a success. Greeted with disappointment or gleeful derision by the critics, it is a book that seems to have succumbed to trendiness. The excitement and energy of *Slaves of New York* is plagiarised in *A Cannibal in Manhattan*, where it becomes a hollow and strained kind of frenzy.

For Tama Janowitz is a victim, albeit a willing one, of the laws of the media: that if they set someone up as a star the chances are that they will then bring them down: from star to shooting star. It is all very well for someone like Sally Beauman, whose first novel was not published when she had just left college, and whose treatment by the critics has never been adulatory, to stress the difference between 'publicity and *self*-publicity'. A writer travels round the country, giving interviews, doing broadcasts, signing copies, having her photograph taken, and the distinction between marketing a book and marketing its author becomes increasingly hazy.

If a young, first-time author is over-hyped, the chances are she will then swiftly be dropped; the effect that this can have upon a writing career can be devastating. The experiences of the literary Brat Pack in the United States testify: Tama Janowitz, Jay McInerney and Brett Easton Ellis have all been set up and knocked down; they have been published too early and exploited by the publishing industry, and are now in danger of becoming have-beens before they reach thirty. These young writers may well have great promise, but with giant cheques, swollen egos and inflated adulation they become personalities who care more about being a writer than about writing, and who cannot cope with critical relegation from the first division.

The Canadian novelist Jane Rule, never set up and never knocked down, and anyway resistant to the glare of limelight, is alert to the dangers of hype, and is careful to resist a media image of herself.

> I do very little publicity. I think you have to be extremely careful that the world doesn't turn you into its terms – I've always said that my business is to write and not to be 'the writer': what the world seems to want of me is to be 'the writer'. The temptation to be successful is in every place in life. I feel very ambivalent about self-publicity because if you live that way then your view of the world gets changed – you get an undue sense of your own importance in the world. And the media does terrible things to people. Once you set them up you have to knock them down. In Australia they say 'we cut our tall poppies down' and in Holland they say 'tall trees get a lot of wind'.

Jane Rule is resolute in her modest ambitions and her desire to live an ordinary and private life, and genuine about caring more about the solitary and self-disciplined act of writing than about the clarion call of wealth and fame. She emphasises the distinction between a hyped writer and a good one. A hyped writer may or may not be talented – she is first and foremost a product of the consumer culture in which we live. She is an object for the public to look to and, fleetingly, admire. As a well-packaged personality who can speak fluently and look attractive on television, she can be made into the flavour of the month.

As the Irish writer Leland Bardwell pointed out, 'We don't have plain people on television.' She considers herself not 'good media meat'. Interviewers label her as a 'great character', which she interprets as a euphemism for 'the kind of person whom children run away from in the streets'. And being good media meat sells books. Mary Gordon is a writer of depth and engaging nuances, and also an attractive woman. She always gets reviewed by *The New York Review of Books*, usually flagged by a large

photograph of herself. Fay Weldon's attractive manner and ready wit is just what radio and television producers want. Maggie Gee admits that perhaps the jacket photograph of herself on *Dying in Other Words* might have helped the unusual amount of attention her first novel received. 'I looked like an insane blonde chihuahua, with lots of diamanté and a strategically placed CND badge' – although as she then says, 'that could have gone either way.'

Sara Maitland puts the case succinctly:

> I think one has to make two separate things, as one does with clothes and painting and with every other designer-craft. There is stuff that is super-hype and there is stuff that is good. Occasionally the two come together but they don't have to and if they do it is merely incidental. You just have to know what is being bought. If you are paid a massive amount of money for a first novel you are being bought for a hype. If you also want to be a novelist you just have to roll with the punches. Now that might be an awfully hard thing to say to someone who is twenty-two. But I would say there is nothing wrong with hype in itself – the only thing that is wrong is assuming that if you are paid more than x, say, then you are better than they are. You may just have a straighter nose or a prettier name or the right subject matter.

Prizes: first among equals

Prize-giving has done much to draw new readers into 'serious' fiction and to give needed and deserved acclaim, financial assistance and encouragement to writers. It can also cement and glaze an already elitist and homogenised writing culture – what Jane Rule calls 'cottage cheese' culture.

The importance of prizes can hardly be exaggerated. Take the British Booker Prize. Publishers plan around it, Christmas shopping is simplified by it, list editors' careers can be made by backing the winner and previously little-known authors can be granted fairy-tale prestige and wealth once the winning label is stamped on to their book's jacket. Of course, in the promotional glare – bets placed at Ladbroke's, the televised dinner, the extensive interviews, the thrill of suspense – the real winner is Booker. The international food and agricultural business pays out a mere £15,000 prize money plus the annual publicity and administrative expenses – and in return receives an hour or so prime time television and sustained attention from the press worldwide.

First sponsored in 1969 and first televised ten years later, the Booker Prize gradually distinguished itself from the other 200 or so literary prizes. When John Berger, 1972 winner, criticised Booker McConnell's trading record in the Caribbean and donated half his prize money to the Black Panthers, his attack ironically helped to hoist the event out of its literary ghetto and on to the front of the news pages – where it has since remained. When Anthony Burgess lost to William Golding in 1980 and refused to accept defeat like an Englishman and gentleman, it proved itself a wonderful television spectacle, combining the adrenalin of the race, the glamour of competing personalities and the familiarity of prize-giving day.

There can be little doubt that the Booker Prize has also succeeded in increasing the readership of serious fiction. It is impossible to measure by how much, but Graham C. Greene thinks that 'with its business of gossip and plotting' it has helped 'the resurrection of serious fiction'.

The shortlist of six has that useful if fiercely unjust function of giving us a recommended reading list from the tens of thousands of novels published each year. And the subsequent impact on sales justifies the Booker Prize's position as the pivot of the publishing year; the jewel in the crown for publishers and authors. Those books considered for the prize are categorised as 'literary' – meaning highbrow, not for mass consumption and therefore not usually very profitable. A hypothetical second novel that follows a respectfully reviewed first novel could normally expect a print-run of around 4,000 copies. The effect on sales if it then went on to win the Booker Prize would be dramatic and immediate. In 1982 Thomas Keneally's *Schindler's Ark* had sold just under 4,500 copies on the eve of the award. A year later UK and Commonwealth sales had reached 56,000 hardback and 250,000 in paperback. In 1983 the surprise winner, J. M. Coetzee's *The Life and Times of Michael K*, had sold 2,500 before the announcement; two months later it had sold 42,000 in hardback alone.

That is only the beginning. When Anita Brookner won the 1984 Booker Prize with *Hotel du Lac* she was a respected but shadowy author whose previous novels had sold no more than 5,000 copies in hardback each. Since the award, Granada Paperbacks have reprinted their backlist Brookners several times. And she is now the centre of attention on review pages.

Everyone agrees that to have one winner is arbitrary and unfair – but the appeal of the Booker Prize resides precisely in choosing a 'first among equals'. The changing fortunes of the Whitbread Prize bear out the point. In 1971 there were five prizes going to five category winners: fiction, first novel, biography, children's book and poetry. The winners received muted media attention. In 1985 Whitbread additionally selected an overall winner from those categories and it was that, rather than prize money amounting to £25,000, which gave it increased status and glamour. Hardly anyone could name its past category winners. Many, however, could identify Douglas Dunn's *Elegies*, Kazuo Ishiguro's *An Artist of the Floating World* or Christy Nolan's *Under the Eye of the Clock* as the 1985, 1986 and 1987 winners.

The sales figures for these winners emphasise Whitbread's higher profile; Dunn's collection of poetry had a print-run in the spring of 1985 of 5,000; in November Faber reprinted a further 2,500 in response to the sales-creating rumour that it would win the poetry category prize; following the announcement two months later that it had won the overall award the publishers reprinted a further 7,200 in January and 4,800 in February. This is extraordinarily successful for a book of poetry. The difficulty of the revamped Whitbread Prize is comparing unlike with unlike – but that is also its appeal. Someone wins. As the TV cameras beam in on one jubilant smile and five stiff upper lips, we realise that too many lose. The losers include not only all those writers who have been passed by, but also all the readers who fall for the myth of the 'best'.

Jeanette Winterson won the 1985 Whitbread First Novel Award with her *Oranges Are Not The Only Fruit*. It was during the lunch to announce the nominations that she began fully to appreciate the inherent sexism of the literary establishment, which is so well represented by the prize system, and the paranoia of some women writers, who are so dismissed by many critics.

I noticed idly that only one of the five categories (mine) had more than one woman on the panel of three judges. The poetry panel had no women at all. When my little chap stood up to present the award he made it clear, without being downright rude, that the book was not his choice but that of the women. He even got my name wrong. In one rambling sentence he humiliated me and called into question the critical ability of his co-judges.

Penelope Fitzgerald won the Booker Prize in 1979 with her novel *Offshore*, having been previously shortlisted with her novel *The Book Shop*. She is amusing about her Booker experiences, but, like Jeanette Winterson, mocks many of its premises.

When *The Book Shop* got on the shortlist I was with Duckworth and I said to my editor, 'What is this Booker Prize, anyway?' I didn't know what it was all about. He just said, 'Oh well, it is this prize where you and I have to go along and we have to wear a dinner jacket or dress – and I haven't got a dinner jacket, though fortunately my cousin has.' Really, we neither of us had a clue. I went along to the dinner with one of my daughters. We neither of us owned dinner dresses and I had to have a bag as well you know – so I bought myself a sponge bag and went with that.

The next year I was with Collins and *Offshore* won it

that year. We were staggered. Another daughter came
with me that year and I still had the sponge bag. That was
the first year that Booker decided that they wouldn't say
until the last minute who had won – there's a very
childish element in all of this, you see. There is something
faintly ridiculous about it. When *The Book Shop* was
shortlisted we all had to line up and it was just like being
at an old-fashioned primary school – everyone was given
a leather-bound copy of their work. I was just behind
Kingsley Amis and when he was given his leather-bound
copy he gave a slight bow – and I thought, 'This is
ludicrous.' But Booker McConnell obviously thought
that this was the way you should treat authors.

Penelope Fitzgerald admits that winning the prize 'made all the
difference' to her. The money then was 'only £10,000 – but that
was a vast sum to me in those days – well, it still is'. She also
thinks that it 'overbalances the whole publishing year' and
'although I'm a beneficiary I'm very doubtful about its effect'.

Well she might be. Whatever the merit and originality of the
individual winners and runners-up, the tone set by Booker is one
of conservatism and caution, and often seems to demonstrate the
stranglehold of the literary establishment. When in 1985 the
Maori writer Keri Hulme won with *The Bone People*, the
announcement was greeted with astonishment, disapproval and
some jubilation. Her three feminist editors, who collected the
prize on her behalf, wove their way to the platform chanting in
Maori and magnificently disrupting the sober and civilised
atmosphere. *The Bone People* started as a short story and then,
over twelve years, 'warped into a novel'. It is a long, exploratory,
volatile tale of three people caught up in love and violence; of
Maori myths and a sense of rootedness; of child abuse and
near-madness; of death, violence, sheer grief, the power of
language and of compassion. *The Bone People* was turned down
by three publishers. Long, untidy, unashamedly displaying the
ragged seams and rips of its long gestation ('I want to have things
rough, cracked open for the reader') it baffled editors. Raw,

passionate and wrinkled with strange words and images, it contradicted the canons of literary good taste. Only thanks to the efforts of the specially formed feminist publishing co-operative Spiral Collective did it ever get published – and then on paper as thin and cheap as toilet paper. It was made abundantly clear that *The Bone People* won the Booker Prize because the judges could not agree; it was their collective third choice.

Keri Hulme exultantly broke through the barriers of the establishment. For a brief moment the Booker award wore a bold countenance: it was not the arbiter of 'good taste' but the enabler of literature that, however flawed, was innovative and audacious and explosively passionate. That has not been the case in other years. In 1984 Anita Brookner won the prize with her immaculate and poignant *Hotel du Lac*. In the same year Angela Carter's *Nights at the Circus* was not even shortlisted. To choose the exquisitely written but slight romance over Carter's stunning tale of magic and desire (and over the broader canvasses and more ambitious subjects of the other shortlisted books) seemed to many a baffling act of cowardice. Sara Maitland, whose admiration for Angela Carter's achievements is unstinting, is vitriolic about the 1984 judgment:

> To give that prize, the year they had that [Carter's] book, to Anita Brookner – now that is a demonstration of philistinism. We must live in a philistine culture when a modest and mean-minded book about the uninteresting immoralities of a class which is dead on its feet as far as culture goes can win . . . yes, that says a lot.

She may be unfair in her scorching attack on Brookner. But look at the 1987 shortlist: Penelope Lively's winning *Moon Tiger*, Nina Bawden's *Circles of Deceit*, Chinua Achebe's *The Anthills of the Savannah*, Peter Ackroyd's *Chatterton*, Iris Murdoch's *The Book and the Brotherhood* and Brian Moore's *The Colour of Blood*. They are not – apart perhaps from Achebe's novel – books to get excited about. And few people claim that any of them were the 'best' books published in 1987. In the numerous Christmas round-ups of contributors' favourite publications of the year the six shortlisted novels were mainly conspicuous by their absence.

In 1988 people complained about what had been left out rather than included. The shortlist was unusual for its solid merit – Peter Carey's fantastic, picaresque and exuberant *Oscar and Lucinda*, David Lodge's warm and sharply observed *Nice Work*, Marina Warner's intricately structured and richly rhetorical *The Lost Father*, Penelope Fitzgerald's understated and unpredictable gem, *The Beginning of Spring*, Bruce Chatwin's oddly arresting *Utz*, and Salman Rushdie's bizarre, magnificent and almost unreadable *The Satanic Verses*. The list included previous winners (Penelope Fitzgerald and Salman Rushdie) and previously shortlisted authors (David Lodge and Peter Carey); there were no dark horses, no rank outsiders – and *Oscar and Lucinda*, the 9–4 favourite, won. Complaints that the shortlist and prize were predictable seem contrary; they were only predictable because selected on merit. What the 1988 shortlist does emphasise, however, is how the lottery of the prize (of all prizes) is rigged in advance. In apparently deliberate contrast with the 'middlebrow' 1987 panel of judges, 1988's male-dominated panel was a highly literary bunch – the Chair Michael Foot, literary editor of *The Independent* Sebastian Faulkes, literary editor of *The Observer* Blake Morrison, film critic Philip French and novelist Rose Tremaine. The selected six books bear the hallmark of their highbrow taste. *Oscar and Lucinda* would not have won the previous year. The fact that the Booker Prize was, in most people's view, awarded to an outstanding novel in no way diminishes the case against the literary prize system.

Emma Tennant sees the effect of the prize system in this country as far-reaching and damaging. Disarmingly admitting that she may be soured by not having been the beneficiary of a major prize, she thinks that 'you can sometimes open a novel and scent, smell, detect in it the need to be on the Booker shortlist'. She lists her criticisms: writers become over-anxious and self-conscious because they know what a huge difference winning a major prize will make to the sales of their book, and they might even write with one eye on that prize; it strains a writer's relationship with her publisher because 'we can tell precisely how a publisher grades our work by its month of publication, and it is rather like an elaborate Chinese court ritual'.

Clearly prizes awarded to literature have undeniable virtues; but they are double-edged. Prizes financially reward writers, and writers are often in great need of cash. Yet, scanning the list of Booker award winners over the last two decades, few represent the impoverished end of the literary spectrum. They draw readers to 'good' books that otherwise might not have been widely read. They also serve simply to shift a body of readership on to a handful of selected works. They are points of encouragement in the publishing year for editors and authors. They also create an inner sanctum of those worthy of awards. They promote public awareness of literature in general, yet at the same time perpetuate an anti-aesthetic of novels in competition, as 'best' or second or unplaced. And the major prizes simply do not heed the literary adventures and experiments which are by their nature risk-takers.

The Feminist Book Fortnight

The Feminist Book Fortnight attempts to give a feminist focus to the publishing year, otherwise so dominated by the major prizes. It was born out of dissatisfaction with the way in which feminist writing is poorly reviewed or not reviewed at all, pushed to the fringes, and avoided by retailers. And it has been successful at many different levels. A great many readers, from all over the world, have been made aware of the strengths, diversity and internationalism of women's writing; main retailers have been forced to recognise, belatedly, that there really are a lot of women readers out there and that feminism can also be commercial. The Fortnight has become an international forum for feminist debate – and sometimes fierce argument.

The Feminist Book Fortnight has undoubtedly been good for women's writing and has now become part of the publishing calendar. Complaints that it has been 'appropriated' by shops like W.H. Smiths are a signal of its success in reaching a wider audience. There are more sophisticated anxieties. Although the organisers are careful to avoid the linear competitiveness of the major awards, calling the books that they choose to highlight during that fortnight not the 'top' but the 'selected' twenty, yet the Feminist Book Fortnight can be for some women what Alison Fell, self-confessed introvert, calls 'Paranoia Book Fortnight': not to be asked to read and talk at the various venues around the country can be very painful. But she also says that if you are one of the included women then you are forced to be 'your own self-publicist and to be set within the category of feminist writers'.

And Alison Fell expresses the dilemma that besets the Fortnight and plagues many writers who are feminist: 'I'm not a feminist writer: I know I'm a feminist; I know I'm a writer. But I'm also Scottish and also a socialist. I don't like the two things stuck together.'

This fear of labels is the thorn in the side of the Feminist Book Fortnight – many women are not included because, while avowedly feminist, they do not write explicitly feminist books – though they do write books shaped by gender consciousness. But explicitly feminist books can sometimes be polemical and spiked by their own good intentions. There have been several fascinating and unpredictable books chosen for the Selected Twenty – but also many distressingly bad ones, in which the imagination is stifled, and which are dictated to, rather than informed by, feminism. Such books translate a liberating theory into a constricting aesthetic. Their writers are fettered by an ideology, and they do no service to the promotion of feminist literature.

The first Feminist Book Fortnight, held in Britain in 1984, was an open, angry and exciting meeting between women writers – and their readers – from all over the world. More recently, it has risked becoming a slightly complacent and sealed-off literary event, serving its own kind of literary establishment. This is a shame, for the great achievement of the Fortnight – and its great distinction from other literary happenings during the year – has been its inclusion of the reader.

Women not only buy and borrow more books than men, they

also bring an excitement and emotional commitment to literature, especially to literature by women. They tend to experience the fictions they are reading at both an intellectual and an emotional level, in a way unusual among male readers, and they have been loyal to feminist presses in a way that has surprised retailers, amazed the mainstream, baffled some critics and annoyed some male writers. Dale Spender recalls hearing an Australian writer, Gerard Windsor, actually accusing women readers of a 'conspiracy' to buy women's writing. When Toni Morrison was signing copies of her latest novel at the feminist Silver Moon bookshop in London, queues of women stretched down Charing Cross Road. Both in the United States and in Britain readings and talks by women writers are almost always well attended and often sold out. Women want not only to read more books by women, they want to know about their lives. The Feminist Book Fortnight was exciting and challenging precisely because the woman reader was not bypassed in the exchange between writers and publishers and critics, but treated and respected as a participator. If it comes to exclude them, it will become just another literary event.

Being just another literary event means jostling with all the numerous literary events to shape and influence the publishing year. The numerous book fairs and prizes exemplify the advantages and the dangers of a promotion-driven, hype-ridden and image-drenched book world. They bring more readers to literature, but only to a carefully and often cautiously selected literature. While they do serve to promote books, they usually promote a certain kind of book, which belongs to the mainstream and does not stray from established literary good taste. Prizes usually give financial reward to writers who least need it. They are welcome, but unfair, laying down standards for the public and for aspiring authors and dedicated to the promotion of culture. They are also a demonstration of cultural competition and philistinism. With their glamour and their inherent conservatism, they neatly express the ambivalence that many feminists and socialists feel about promotion, packaging and design.

three

WRITING COMMUNITIES

Writing is surrounded by glamour and mystery; it is the most solo of arts, and reading the most single of pleasures. Writers must work on their own and their only real tool is their imagination. The traditional image of the writer – starving in a garret, wasting from consumption, sacrificing all for art – is not easily thrown off. It is an image which many writers carry with them. Penelope Fitzgerald, for example, still thinks of writers as large men with broad-brimmed hats and curved pipes. It is also an image which encourages writers to accept bad treatment and poverty, confirming but romanticising their solitude.

Although self-help groups have proliferated over the last decade, most writers rely upon more informal and emotionally supportive networks. In spite of literary gossip and malice, it is astonishing how few struggling writers envy their wealthy colleagues, even while they resent the jackpot mentality of the star system. Emma Tennant admitted that 'you would have to be a Mother Superior' not to feel twinges of jealousy, but many others insisted that writers had chosen a precarious occupation and deserved every penny they got.

Fellow loyalty, usually subsuming most of the gleeful literary bitchiness, supports the author, but at the same time emphasises the 'specialness' of writing. Writers often seem to relish the loneliness of being set apart; isolation is countered by living in a sealed-off world of literary gossip, competition and fellowship.

Writing programmes in the United States

In the United States there does exist a formal and rapidly growing form of support for writers, which clarifies the exclusiveness of literary coteries and trends. When, in 1987, Deborah Futter of Bantam Press in New York won the Tony Godwin Fellowship (awarded in the UK and the States to an 'outstanding young editor') and spent a few weeks in London with Bloomsbury Publishing, she reflected upon the differences between the two countries' publishing industries. Apart from the obvious difference in scale, she pointed to the lack of support for new writers in Britain:

> Where are the young writers, the first novelists, the
> authors who we in New York are competing like mad to
> discover, publish and establish? Where in London are the
> writing programmes that nurture them? Why is there not
> the same driving desire we in the States have to discover –
> and then to convert to media darling-dom – new talent?

In America writing programmes are a big industry, getting bigger, while in Britain they scarcely exist. In America these programmes are a large source of income for universities, and they do not simply encourage young talent, they act as well-oiled doors into the publishing world. No longer do the aspiring writers have to slog away in isolation to produce a manuscript, find an agent or send the notorious brown envelope to half the publishing houses in America. At the writing programmes the student writer can find, rolled into the one person of the teacher, a critic and encourager, a surrogate agent, an introduction to a friendly publisher, an admiring puff for the back of the book when it is brought out and access to a network of like-minded writers. It is a world of networking and power-broking. If a student manages to get on to one of the more eminent courses, taught by a well-known author, then they are halfway to literary success. The writing programmes have thrown up coteries, clustered around the big name teacher-writer (Richard Ford,

Caroline Fourchet . . .), which produce certain genres of writing.

Deborah Futter of Bantam pointed to the virtues of the American system: encouragement of young writers, access to an otherwise closed world of publishing, a pool of budding talent in which editors can go fishing for first novels, a network of writers that can break down the isolation of writing. But Deborah Baker of Overlook expressed the simultaneous anxieties of a large number of North American editors, seeing the boom in writing programmes as a 'process' that produces 'processed' literature.

> Writing programmes are a big source of income for a lot of universities. For some reason they have an endless supply of people who dream of being writers. There is this network and they are all jockeying for position in the sense of the student writer getting published or the writing teacher getting published. They are really plugged into all of that – wanting to attract students to their programmes, and therefore in the business of supplying blurbs for their students, supplying agents for their students, supplying editors for their students.

Giving as an example the recent anthologies from particular writing schools, she says:

> The feeling I have is that these writing programmes have created a homogenised writing culture that is not necessarily regional. It tends to be focused on contemporary life and contemporary mores and behaviour and immediate adolescent collegiate experience. I'm astounded by it – and I don't welcome it when it comes in manuscript after manuscript on to my desk. In fact, I feel really very testy about it; I feel like lecturing people on grammar.

She points out that there are probably fifty students every two years who are trying to become novelists out of a typical university – and there is at least one writing programme in every state.

Deborah Baker was unequivocal about the narrowing effect that writing programmes have upon young aspiring writers. They encourage bright young people who tend to produce novels about their immediate collegiate experience. Their cultural heroes are the writers featured in *Vanity Fair*. They do not, complain editors who are bombarded with their manuscripts about the banality of urban life, seem to have read Faulkner or Melville; their minds seem 'closed to larger themes'. Deborah Baker believes that the rise of the young trendy writer reflects North American culture today:

> The United States is very much focused on itself; it encourages self-interest and self-aggrandisement and self-indulgence and that narcissistic, blinkered perspective. Like Reagan, who is the way an old person often is, the writing programmes tend to produce literature that is completely in the present, responding to things as they come but not remembering from one minute to the next what went on before.

This a-historical, self-concerned literature, which has caught the imagination of North American readers by reflecting and glorifying their individual lives and anxieties, is very much a product of writing programmes. It is fashionable, image-conscious literature.

Writing programmes in the United States can homogenise the established literary scene, excluding writers who do not belong. Barbara Wilson is a writer of lesbian feminist novels and editor of the fringe Seal Press. She feels that the networks function through exclusivity, macho values and a male club mentality.

> There are waves that come out of writing schools – there was the minimalist wave, for example. It is all about networking really, so if you are pegged early and you've got a sponsor and you go to a writing school, then you are going to have a teacher who has publishing contacts

65

and you'll go to writing conferences where you will be pushed forward and maybe given a chance to read. And the editors of some of the bigger magazines will be there and they'll have a cosy chat with you and then you will send your stuff to them and then they will publish it and then New York editors will see your name and write to you . . . it is all like that. And that is a big problem for people who aren't part of it, who aren't 'in', who don't live somewhere like New York, who aren't part of a writing programme. However good they are, it is so difficult to break into.

Lesbian and feminist writers tend to be excluded from the smoothed path to success. They are not on the circuit, do not know the right people, do not have the right subjects, do not have the kind of face that fits, are not prepared to put up with the sexual harassment that often goes on. A writer like Rebecca Brown, now living in London because she would have 'dropped down the drain' if she had stayed in her home town of Seattle, heartily dislikes the 'expanded college magazine' atmosphere of the writing schools, and denounces the literature they enable as 'all a ready-made package of culture'.

Writing has pre-eminently been a middle-class occupation, ostensibly open to all but often barred to those who could not afford the time or who did not have the contacts and move in the right milieu. Writing programmes might appear to open up the world of literature to a greater number and variety of people, but in America they actually serve to formalise the structures of privileged access, shutting out those people who have always been shut out. While the young and eminently hypeable college graduates produce a steady stream of new wave literature – 'very cool, very minimal and very brittle' according to Mary Cunnane – there are, of course, other less classifiable novels that are being written and that triumph. Toni Morrison's rise to bestseller status with the stunning *Beloved* is a sign that literary miracles still succeed. But writing programmes shore up prevailing systems. They exile those outside the network, and ensure that fringe publishers and authors remain fringe.

Community groups in the United Kingdom

In Britain such systems simply do not operate in the same way. There are a few creative writing courses, most notably at East Anglia. But any networks that do exist remain informal. Apart from what Maureen Duffy calls the DIY groups – the Writer's Guild, the authors' pressure groups that have pushed for Minimum Terms agreements from publishers and Copyright and Public Lending Rights – writing groups have tended to be small, unofficial and supportive groups evolving from the need of certain sections of the writing population to find a voice previously unheard.

Women's writing groups have proliferated over the past fifteen years, largely thanks to the efforts of the Workers' Educational Association, the Federation of Worker Writers and Community Publishers. Many women for the first time have access not only to group support but also to a low-cost production and distribution system. Brighton's Queenspark Women Writers' Group is an example of a successful community publishing enterprise, which gives women the confidence to write, and control over production. Community publishing has developed out of the class bias of publishing. It gives working-class women a forum where none previously existed and transforms working-class women's writing from an uncharted territory and hidden pleasure into something which is publicly acknowledged. It could not be further from the highly developed, commercial and hypeable writing programmes in the States: it benefits precisely those people who are excluded from writing schools – working-class women, older people, those who have missed out on formal education, those who lack the background and confidence of the traditional literary elites.

Community publishing does not open a door into mainstream publishers, nor does it hold out promises of wide readerships, wealth and sudden glamorous fame. Modest, low-key and local, it is the complete antithesis to the world of takeovers and wild advances. However, the value of such publishing lies in stripping the mystique from the act of writing, and of encouraging those

people who are usually denied a means of self-articulation to realise the individual importance of their own lives. While some of the collections brought out by Queenspark Women Writers' Group are very engaging, and some revealing about the lives of so-called 'ordinary' women, they are rarely of great literary merit. Community publishing groups have not traditionally spilt over into mainstream presses, in the way that other fringe presses have done. Their value is modest, self-sufficient and small-scale. For most of the community authors, it is the act of *writing* their lives that is significant, rather than the fact that their lives can be transformed into fiction and read by others.

The *Tales I Tell My Mother* group represents a fine example of what a collaborative writing collective can do and the extensive value it can possess. In the mid-1970s five women – Zoë Fairbairns, Valerie Miner, Michèle Roberts, Sara Maitland and Michelene Wandor – formed a writing group. Eighteen months later, after much discussion about issues raised as women writers, feminists and socialists, fifteen short stories were ready for publication. The collection was not simply a collective effort but a unique experiment in collaborative writing, breaking away from the romantic isolation of the writer and challenging a traditional view of fiction. *Tales I Tell My Mother* rebuts the glamorous isolation of the creative work and in that sense it was a political as well as imaginative experiment – which might be the reason that it was rejected by nineteen publishers, including feminist ones, before being taken on by the new and very small Journeyman Press.

Tales I Tell My Mother launched the five women on their writing careers: all went on to achieve significant literary success. Of course it is not possible to tell what they would have done without their mutually supportive beginnings, but the writing group was a fertile soil. Its effect was the very opposite to that of the American writing programmes; it did not provide access to the publishing world and it did not encourage a genre of writing; rather it bred a creative diversity.

The working-class women's groups and the group which produced *Tales I Tell My Mother* break down some of the barriers between writers and non-writers, and reject the individualistic mystique of writing. They do so by making it into a collaborative and community exercise, in which the process of learning and sharing is emphasised. Joan Riley, the Caribbean writer, would applaud such practical experiments in sharing. In her native country sharing is a natural way of behaving in the community, but she argued vehemently that in Britain we hardly know the meaning of the word – and hence cannot be said to live in real communities at all.

Joan Riley has experienced isolation, both as a writer and as a self-exile from Jamaica. She has described it vividly in *The Unbelonging*, her first novel, which is about the harsh realities of immigrant life in Britain. The novel's central character, Hyacinth, exchanges the warmth and exuberance of the Caribbean for the gloom and hostility of inner-city life. She becomes a stranger in both her old and new homes. Joan Riley is less bleak about her own exile, emphasising her rich cultural inheritance rather than her subsequent loss. She was born in St Mary, Jamaica, the youngest of eight children, and her mother died in childbirth. But, she says, it was not a 'misspent youth: my father gave me a real consciousness of myself and of my history and my people. And a love of people.' She is bitter about the way that immigrants to Britain have been stripped of this sense of community and denied their culture: 'everyone needs a past to have the chance of a future'.

Joan Riley is distressed by 'the blighting of black people in Britain', and disillusioned with the left. They, 'with their liberal and guilt-ridden consciences', have created a 'non-person with a problem – a thing called a black, with a problem called racism' and have 'defined in us an oppression which is the equivalent of original sin'. Yet Joan Riley shares with many of her community a resourcefulness and resilience that leads her to say, 'I live inside my skin. It doesn't really matter where I live. We believe that Africa is wherever you are. It is the culture, tradition and the ability to live with dignity and pride inside your own skin.'

It is because of her sense of a shared culture and her involvement in her immediate Caribbean community that Joan Riley dismisses the mystique of writing with such vigour.

> I think it comes from the time when the actual knowledge locked up in books was a form of privilege and power, and the people who could provide that were seen as special. People still have an idea about books – their truth and their greatness. It is hard to break down, for there is a sense of adequacy in being 'above the common herd'. The writer is sentimentalised and neglected – and yet who were the first writers? People who could afford to be – writing was not something that people like me were supposed to practise; writing was for middle-class people who could afford to be gaunt-looking in a garret, who were married to someone in a good job or who had sufficient capital; who could say after university, 'I think I'll just take a year off and go to Southern France and see how it goes;' who are thought of as pure and aren't going to go out there into the community and get their feet mucky.

But, she insists,

> Take me out of my community and I am finished as a writer. OK, I can still craft a book but what is in it? I think of it as all of us walking along a road, and everybody else stops to look at something, but I walk further on. I cross the bridge but then the bridge falls down. It doesn't mean that because I crossed the bridge I am better than you, who didn't. I just happened to get over it before it fell down. Let's rebuild it and then you can walk across as well. But most writers don't feel that – they like to face the world across a great divide. They might mouth 'oh yes, everybody can write' but they don't really believe it because that would devalue their work. I know that everybody has a story to tell.

Writers reading writers

While women writers frequently voiced their sense of unbelonging and their role as the solitary and unrooted observer, most felt that they did belong to a community of women readers. As writers, they are isolated; as readers of women writers, they find models, influences and forms of encouragement that draw them into an invisible but powerful network and give them a sense of extensive comradeship.

Several women said that they actually began to write because they discovered women's writing. The Irish writer Mary Lavin always adored reading, but it was only when she realised that the subject of her PhD, Virginia Woolf, was a living writing woman – rather than a name on a book – that she dashed off her first short story. Alison Fell stumbled across the Brontës and understood that serious literature by women could be exciting and relevant. The American post-modernist writer Leslie Dick says that Virago's reprints in the 1970s were a literary and emotional revelation that pushed her into creating fiction herself. The prolific American writer Joyce Carol Oates insists that she could never have written about the diverse and depressed lives of Americans had she not consumed all the classic realist novels by women. When the women's presses started to publish forgotten works, the hungry response showed how much we needed to know our common language and cultural inheritance. Feminist publishers revealed to women readers a literary and cultural continuity that had been neglected.

More particularly, the women who started writing in the 1950s and 1960s have so encouraged and influenced subsequent generations of writers that they are almost the mothers of contemporary women's novels. Figures like Doris Lessing, Iris Murdoch and Margaret Drabble in Britain, and Marge Piercy in the United States, wrote about women's lives in ways which combined private and public issues, and personal and national anxieties. Their stature demonstrated that not only could women write as well, or better, than their male contemporaries, they could also write about any subject they pleased. Antonia Byatt remembers the exhilaration that she felt when first reading Iris Murdoch, who 'taught me that women did not have to write about small issues'. And Doris Lessing, in her introduction to the reprinted *The Golden Notebook*, writes that she was amazed by the number of letters she received from women, expressing gratitude to her for so illuminating the large politics of their personal lives.

The grateful women readers who become respected women writers often repay their debts to their forerunners by actively supporting younger or less established women writers. Zoë Fairbairns regularly attends readings and talks by her female contemporaries, not just out of genuine interest, but also because she wants to support them. Like many women, her reaction to newly emerging talent is not jealousy or a feeling of vulnerable rivalry, but a real delight that another woman seems to be overcoming the difficulties of starting out as a writer. Women writers may not have the helpful encouragement of wives or secretaries, but they do often enter the elastic community of other women writers.

Self-exile

It is unexpected when a writer feels a sense of belonging. Many see themselves as the outsiders of their age; many feel that the state of unbelonging actually unfetters their creative imagination. Ideological or literal homelessness coincides with literary freedom; loneliness with imaginative resourcefulness.

The Indian writer Anita Desai, who hates the 'inequalities, melodrama and noisy violence' of her country and who is regarded by Indians as 'eccentric', thinks that only as an Indian outsider can she write for her scattered and non-Indian audience. She is the daughter of an Indian father and a German mother, whose inheritance as well as her chosen profession distances her from her people. While regretting her disaffection for India and admitting to her loneliness there – her only real friend is Ruth Prawer Jhabvala, who is also an outsider in her own country – Anita Desai realises the advantages it has for her writing. She is able to mediate her country, explaining it to a non-Indian audience, gathering up its violent disjunctions in a cool prose that always teeters on the edge of violence itself. She is intimately involved with Indian life, and cannot conceive living and writing elsewhere, and yet she depicts India as an observer, and consistently returns to the theme of exile and unbelonging. Writing at one remove from her country gives her fiction a width and internationalism it would otherwise not have.

Similarly, many Australian women writers inhabit a cultural contradiction. They are often fiercely rooted in the landscape, history and culture of their country, and yet they do not have a recognisable Australian readership. Australia is a country of only 16 million, almost half of whom are post-war immigrants. Within such a cosmopolitan population, it is impossible to assume a common cultural tradition or to write for a particular audience, in the way that it is possible in a small and dense country like Britain. And so, while many women write of particular Australian themes or locations, many struggle to avoid national or parochial issues. The sly erotic novels of Elizabeth Jolley, which occupy the hinterland of fantasy, could come from almost any country. Jessica Anderson merges the particular with the universal. Kate Grenville chooses to narrate, in her novel funded by the Australian bicentenary celebrations, the entire history of her country. There are still Australian novels that cannot travel beyond their own backyards – tales set on Bondi Beach, for example – expecting the reader to be familiar with the trends and vocabulary of that particular area. But where British novels have often been cosily ensconced in the literary traditions and cultures of Britain, Australian novels lack familiar assumptions and so have largely escaped parochialism.

Other writers expressed the advantages of exile and self-exile. The American Rebecca Brown chooses to live in London because it is 'easier to fabricate myths' away from her background and because being a foreigner 'gives freedom from old patterns of living and writing'. Another American, Leslie Dick, sees her self-exile in the United Kingdom as an advantage for a writer because 'you don't have a set of assumptions belonging to your class or generation'. And Maureen Duffy, an outsider because of her working-class upbringing and middle-class occupation, emphasises the 'existential' self-reliance and self-questioning into which she has been forced. Michèle Roberts has taken on herself the mantle of 'writer-in-exile', moving around Europe, and she spoke of her creative drive as a 'continual search for home and completeness'. Mary Dorcey, the lesbian poet in Southern Ireland, says that she feels one of a generation of 'scandalous women', refusing to leave her country and yet conscious of its constraints. Leland Bardwell, another Irish writer, senses that she is condemned by her rejected Protestant religion to be an outsider in her own country, and this pervades her writing. Elaine Feinstein's Jewish ancestry and horror at what happened in the 1940s haunts her writing with the sense of self-loss.

Feminism as home?

The sense of exile and self-exile, which was frequently voiced by women writers, romanticises their social role (they are the lonely observers) and at the same time rejects parochialism and cosiness.

However, a substantial number of younger writers qualified their feeling of existential loneliness. For many of those who had grown up and come of age during the heady early days of the women's movement, feminism is their sense of belonging. Michèle Roberts is explicit: 'feminism is my only true home, my internal climate' – adding regretfully that sometimes sisters fight within the home and home is not always a tranquil place to be. Zoë Fairbairns says her writing has been defined and 'validated' by feminism: 'I am interested in the politics of relationships between men and women, and because I see them in a certain way, therefore I am a feminist – it is important to get it that way round.' Sara Maitland has described (in a collection of essays edited by Michelene Wandor, *On Gender and Writing*) how she learnt at university that she was 'not cut out to be an academic; that her commitment to stories and her class background would stop her from being like the other young poets; that she was profoundly confused and unhappy; that politics mattered; that being mad was not fun any more; and that men were more boring and more mean than she had been hoping'. Then 'the little girl got lucky.' Like a latter-day Cinderella, 'sitting at home and rather pissed off', she is visited by her fairy godmother, feminism. Feminism transformed all the old things around her – all the old stories took on new meanings – and the little girl suddenly became a woman, and the woman suddenly learnt to be a writer.

And yet many of those women, who came of age with feminism and who are now seeing feminism come of age itself, voice their dissatisfaction with the contemporary feminist debate and with current feminist fiction. Sara Maitland is forthright. Stressing her gratitude to feminism for the way that it 'synchronised' her life and made her into a writer, she is disappointed by how little good fiction the women's movement has produced. 'Neither at the serious and profoundly philosophic level nor at the popular level are we producing really good novels. They are unexciting, they are self-indulgent. I'm sick of brave novels – I'd like to see some really good ones.'

Or, as Dale Spender puts it, 'the more you contemplate your navel, the more fluff you find.'

While in the United States there are writers of stature – Alice Walker, Maya Angelou, Marge Piercy, Louise Erdrich – who take gender and colour and class, the stuff of history, and then fictionalise it, in Britain feminist writers seem to have suffered from a failure of the imagination. Many of the most exciting young British writers are not explicitly feminist. Jeanette Winterson, who has lived most of her adult life under the shadow of Mrs Thatcher, would certainly call herself a feminist – but not a 'feminist writer'. *The Passion*, her novel which heralded a new and important literary talent, is ambitious, grave, exciting, full of a sense of saga and magic; it dares to take the whole world as its stage. But it is not a consciously 'feminist' novel, for it explodes the developed feminist theory that you write out of gender consciousness. *The Passion* is a tremendous book, as welcome as sunshine on the rather drab landscape of new writing in the UK. Feminist in the largest sense of the word, yet it does not come directly from the women's movement. By adopting as her primary narrator a male character, without apology or self-

75

positioning, it implies that gender does not really form consciousness.

Perhaps this is because British and North American feminism itself, as a theory and practice, is stuck in a phase of gloom, fragmentation and defensiveness. Attacked from all sides, wincing under the Conservative backlash, retreating into style and radical chic, it can no longer provide what Michèle Roberts called the 'internal climate' that would enable creativity. Neither fired with dramatic truths, nor reassuringly offering disaffected women a true emotional home, 1980s feminism has tended to produce feminist fiction that is stale with reiterated truths, angst-ridden, confessional, 'brave'. That emphatically does not mean that it has actually hampered writers who might, without it, have written better literature. Feminism has encouraged writers who might never have written at all. It has validated writers who, before they found feminism, felt they had no 'right' to write. It has given a whole new subject area to literature, demonstrating that women's lives are important and their fictions exciting and readable. It has produced presses to publish women's writing. It has encouraged readers who were, often unknowingly, hungry for women's writing. It has meant an enormous increase in the richness and range of fiction. And it has been a vital tool of the women's movement.

But one of the paradoxes and problems that feminist writers have now to confront is the power of their gratitude towards feminism. If the women's movement has been, for many of them, a home, the dangers are obvious. For homes are both places of belonging and places of childhood and adolescence. One of the biggest struggles for any writer is to break away from adolescent into adult writing, discarding -isms.

Homes can be too cosy. They encourage confession; they assume, and they understand, private codes. And feminist novels can also be too cosy, relying on a loyal feminist readership, a set of familiar preoccupations to work over, and a shared and limited vocabulary. While it was necessary to explore the importance of daily and domestic details, centring specifically on female experience, that time should now have passed. Feminism is no longer in

76

its adolescence, and women writers should be able to take it out into the wider world. Remaining with the familiar because what lies beyond the front door is so uncertain is an unsatisfactory reason for not venturing outside.

four

CENSORSHIP AND SELF-CENSORSHIP

In January 1986 the 48th PEN International Congress was held in New York. Its official theme was 'the Writer's Imagination and the Imagination of the State'. Its unofficial theme was the under-representation of women – out of 117 panelists, only one in seven was a woman; among the thirty-two writers who read from their work, only eight were women. Prepared papers dealt with the role of the state in literature, with acts of cultural oppression and with the writer's relationship to his or her country. Unprepared and angry speeches by the women present protested against the 'state of the imagination' of the PEN International Congress 1986. In Margaret Atwood's words, the 14 per cent female presence was 'about as good as the *Oxford Book of Welsh Verse*, which starts in the twelfth century'. She was representing 'an absence'. In spite of the more phobic statements by the then President of PEN, Norman Mailer (claiming that 14 per cent was a fair representation of women's intellectual status, refusing to be 'pussy whipped' by Grace Paley and her supporters), it would be a mistake to think that the lack of women writers was a deliberate policy. Rather, it was a pugnacious version of a prevailing attitude. Writer Cynthia Ozik spoke at the Congress of the writer's wish to 'achieve universal humanitarian expression'. She then quoted Anton Chekhov's belief that 'writers and artists should engage in politics only enough to protect themselves from politics', and added, 'There are times

78

when "only enough" means 100 per cent.'

In Britain or the United States, we do not face the kinds of literal and brutal barriers that writers in other countries have to live with – not, at least, since Senator McCarthy's purge in the United States in the 1950s. The experience of the Russian poet Irina Ratushinskaya, imprisoned as a 'dissident' Christian and released under *glasnost*, is unimaginable for us. The situation with which Nadine Gordimer lives daily in South Africa, as a white and highly respected writer unswervingly opposed to the apartheid regime, is inconceivable. Few books are actively banned in Britain. There have been some well-documented exceptions: the long-drawn-out, expensive and eventually ludicrous legal wrangle over *Spycatcher* and the innocuous and tedious *Jenny Lives with Eric and Martin* are the most obvious. Such exceptions point to a changing climate. The visible signs of censorship are the concrete and ugly manifestations of a society that rejects opposition and seek to shipwreck imaginative truth-telling.

Section 28 of the Local Government Act, which bans local councils in Great Britain from actively 'promoting' homosexuality, passed through Parliament to vocal opposition, but even more to public acclaim. It fed public anxiety about a homosexual 'conspiracy'. During its passage through the House of Commons it became more apparent than ever that hundreds of thousands of people have the same fear of homosexuals as they do of immigrants – that these 'others' of society threaten the stability and 'normality' of the heterosexual majority. Section 28 will probably not be used widely to forbid specific publications. But it does create a feeling of fear and caution among writers, fettering their imaginations. It may not discourage writers from exploring sexual identities, discussing and describing homosexuality, or presenting homosexual relationships in a realistic and positive way. But it does have an effect: it smashes a wedge into the unconscious. Writers may find that instead of writing freely they are writing in opposition to censorship. Moreover, the bigotry behind Section 28 must cast a different angle of light over our society. Fifteen years ago, attitudes were substantially less punitive. We live in a post-AIDS era and our plague mentality is fuelled by picking out and blaming society's 'others'.

The lesson of Section 28 in the United Kingdom, or of the sporadic raids by the Moral Majority in the United States to destroy 'offensive' literature (like *The Grapes of Wrath*), is that specific acts of censorship are born out of and feed into a general climate of prejudice. Censorship is not just an act, it is an attitude. And the ripple effect of specific examples also demonstrates that there are many different kinds of censorship, from the decisively external to the insidiously internal.

The difficulty of freeing the imagination from external and internal censorship has particular problems for many women writers. They fear writing 'polemical' books – a word, or one of its synonyms, which is hurled so often at feminist books in condemnation that the message must be clear: art is not ideo-logical, not gendered, not there to convert. But there is also the fear of writing books that in some way betray feminism – which, after all, enabled many women to start writing. The difficulty of experiencing gender as liberating is profound. For many women writers, particularly those who are explicitly feminist, the way into the uncluttered imagination is crowded with censoring figures, barring the way forward.

There is the Patriarchal Finger-Wagger – he who says, 'I told you so,' at every failure. And the modernised Angel in the House – who for Virginia Woolf in the 1930s was an 'intensely sympa-thetic', 'immensely charming' and 'utterly unselfish' young woman who sacrificed herself and her writing talent daily, and who for many women writing in the late 1980s is a no less dangerous representative of 'ideological correctness'. There is the Priest in the Closet – a formidable lurking presence hidden within many an 'atheist'. There is the Wolf at the Door – the fear of not being able to buy the food or pay the gas bill. And the Child at the Study Door – the difficulty of being committed to both children and writing.

The Patriarchal Finger-Wagger

The Patriarchal Finger-Wagger has been specifically characterised in several books by women. In Frankie Finn's ambitious
Out on the Plain, he is split into two sneering male figures, Mr
Smith and Mr Jones, who sit in complacent judgment upon the
struggling author. In Michèle Roberts's *The Book of Mrs Noah*, he
is The Gaffer (and, it transpires, the author of the Bible), who
interrupts and criticises the tales the Five Sibyls are spinning.
Always, he represents the fear of failure, and always he has to be
dismissed through anger or mockery before the author/narrator
can write.

The Irish poet Mary Dorcey says that of her '2,000' censoring
figures, the most powerful is that of patriarchy. Brought up as a
Catholic in Ireland, where her mother's ambition was that she
should be an air hostess ('because I had narrow hips'), and where
feminism is still regarded by some as a dirty word, she had to
overcome multiple obstacles before writing. It is not only that
her subjects of concern were regarded as unacceptable, but that
she felt 'the act of writing itself is something that men do' – in
some sense, therefore, something that women are not supposed
to do. This is a peculiarly harmful conditioning. It does not
merely mean that it is more difficult for women to be published,
or to think of themselves as writers, or to be accepted as writers
and yet as normal women. It also sets a painfully sprung trap for
feminists in implying that, as soon as they become writers, they
desert their gender – that, in a hazy way, they are no longer really
women at all. Success, in other words, de-genders them, for
success is a male concept.

Such a large and defeating statement might seem exaggerated.
After all, women have been successful as writers ever since they
took up the pen. Nevertheless it is common for even the most
acclaimed women to resist the notion of their success. It is for
many an alien concept; an accolade awarded by male authority.
And it is astonishing how many women writers immediately
respond to the suggestion of success with a spontaneous and
emphatic 'No!' before then carefully re-defining what they meant

by it. Success as doing what they most wanted to do, success as doing whatever they did as well as possible: these are acceptable forms of achievement. But success as status is not. Women talk of the disjuncture between how they are regarded by the outside world and how they regard themselves; image and so-called reality tear at each other, creating a chasm of self-doubt. Many of them know that they have produced good works and deserved recognition, but at the same time they feel that they have pulled off some complicated kind of bluff and self-bluff. Yawning at their feet with each book they embark upon is the abyss of failure – which is also their 'natural', female element.

It is as if many women live at two different levels simultaneously – the level at which they can be confident about their own worth, rationally assessing their performance, and the level at which they are deeply unconfident. Even the brightest moments can then be edged with panic, for 'success' proves nothing of worth but is like a mirage receding with each step. Such insecurity demands external affirmation – and of course that is a problem for writers who work alone and receive affirmation long after their book is completed. Although self-doubt obviously cuts across genders, nevertheless it affects women more noticeably than men. It is Mary Dorcey's figure of patriarchy, censoring her before she even begins to write. It is the 'voice on the shoulder' of fellow Irish writer Leland Bardwell. It is what Zoë Fairbairns calls 'them' but acknowledges is really 'me', to whom she continually has to prove herself.

Another Irish woman, Catherine Brophy, whose first novel, *The Liberation of Margaret McCabe*, was written in her early forties, describes the difficulty she had of thinking of herself as a 'writer'. She expressed the double-edged feeling of confidence and insecurity very clearly:

> After I had written the book, even though it was very
> well reviewed, I had a sort of panic: 'This is only a fluke.'
> I think that is very female, to be continually thinking, 'I
> don't know whether I am good enough.' What always
> got to me most was the very intellectual male who would

go on about literature as if it were some sort of secret that I hadn't got a hold on. My writing was just writing; their writing was Literature. I might have a deep sense that what I am doing is OK but yet I am always afraid to trust to that.

There is a sense that women both take what they are doing extremely seriously, pouring emotional as well as intellectual energy into their writing – and often moral commitment – and at the same time find it difficult to take themselves seriously as writers. This conundrum can gradually squeeze them until writing becomes more and more painful. It can even dry up altogether.

Leland Bardwell, whose poetry and novels have been greeted with praise and respect both in Ireland and in Britain, dreads her recurring inability to write, which she recognises as a loss of faith in her words.

I always think it is the end; with each block I think it is the end. And I do get terribly depressed when I can't write. Especially now that I'm getting older and I think that every minute is precious – that I won't have enough time to say everything that I want to say. I need the nudge before I can start work, but then when I do start it is killing me writing this bloody novel, just killing me, and I'm doing everything to stop going to the typewriter in the morning – you know, cleaning out the range. And then when I get halfway through I ask that terrible question, 'Why?' Why am I writing this? Who wants another book? And if there is no reason you'd better stop and throw the whole lot away. Once that question has come up and I've found, eventually, some kind of answer, then it is downhill all the way. I suppose, vainly, I tell myself that I am doing something that has never been done quite like this before. That it is important.

The Angel in the House

Feminism has encouraged women to turn their backs on the Patriarchal Finger-Wagger. But in some cases it provided in his stead an alternative forbidding figure, far more fearsome because more beloved: the Angel of ideological correctness. Many of the daughters of second-wave feminism undergo the same anguished struggle as literal daughters to break free from their grateful dependence. There may be a period of painful disentanglement before a mature relationship between an individual feminist and her movement can emerge – a relationship in which freedom, criticism and independence are finally possible. The Angel in the House, stooping over the shoulder of the writer with words about 'betrayal' and 'what will they say?', is a figure who belongs to a writer's immaturity. Getting rid of her is a necessarily painful part of growing up. In Virginia Woolf's murderous terms, the Angel must be killed off in an act of self-defence: 'Had I not killed her she would have killed me. She would have plucked the heart out of my writing.'

Like the demise of the Finger-Wagger, the Angel's destruction has been a frequent subject for the feminist literary canon. While patriarchal attitudes and establishment oppressions are a less painful and more popular target, many feminist writers turn to self-examination and self-criticism after the first flush of idealism. The feminist confessional novel, with its anguished analysis of motives and its pursuance of independence and true freedom, often has at its centure the flushing out of the Angel, whose hold over the imagination is for many feminists far more tenacious than any of the more obvious forms of censorship. In fact, it seems that for some women writers it is almost impossible to write a novel that does not have, as its sub-text and shadow-subject, the escape of the author/narrator from her murderous Angel of Correctness. But making her into a central protagonist in the feminist literary canon can have the paradoxical and sometimes crippling effect of validating her by recognising her continuing dominance.

Alison Fell's first novel for adults, *Every Move You Make*, was the necessary writing-out of her conflicting feelings about the feminist and left-wing politics of the 1970s. Taking as its subject the process of unshackling the self from received ideologies, it tells the story of June Guthrie, Scottish and working-class, an idealistic and insecure child of the 1970s counterculture, who is torn between reflection and action, utopianism and compromise, autonomy and dependence. The novel deals with the betrayals as well as the liberations of the heady days of early feminism and political utopianism. June's own fears are mirrored by her author's, for Alison Fell wrote the book out of 'terror that I would get trashed'. And, sure enough, she did:

> because if you are on the left it is as if you are not allowed
> to have any criticisms; you've got to keep the show on
> the road and protect the left. So I found that all my left
> loyalties were questioned and that I had to untie myself
> from left groups and ideologies.

Not only was *Every Move You Make* regarded by some as an act of betrayal, but Alison Fell was haunted by a sense of betrayal as she wrote it.

Because the novel works through internal conflicts in a process of giving permission to its author, it is appealing, brave but ultimately unsatisfactory. It is too self-concerned to last beyond the short age in which it was written. *Every Move You Make* is a novel of its time and for its time (about the 1970s, published in the early 1980s). It captures a feminist uncertainty about motivation and puritanism, and a certain kind of obsession about the kinds of internal conditioning that women have to deal with once they have struggled with the Patriarch.

The struggle of the author/narrator to break free of self-censoring presences is also a central concern in Michèle Roberts's fictions. True emotional (and, simultaneously, writerly) independence signals a coming of age for both writer and character, and replaces a more traditional happy-ever-after. From the realism of her early novels to the more symbolic *The Wild Girl* and *The Book of Mrs Noah* she has grappled with the definitions and difficulties of feminism. Indeed, they are increasingly self-referential – *Mrs Noah* is soaked in the myths, metaphors and wrangles of feminist theories. Five Sibyls (who are also five writers) gather on an Ark (which is also a vast library, a suburban house, a nuclear shelter, a coffin and a womb, a vision of the future and a representation of the past) to talk about sex, clothes, friendship, food, the writer's block, lovers, husbands and children, the meaning of life. Michèle Roberts describes it as a novel that 'celebrates future possibilities' but it also represents, like Alison Fell's novel, a kind of 1970s feminism: preoccupied with meaning and re-definition; full of angst and interiority; endlessly referential. It succumbs to the very clichés it attacks, and the intellectual habits it deplores. The Angel, chased round and round the Ark, becomes a sixth Sibyl.

Zoë Fairbairns is more robust about the Angel in the House. She admits that 'sometimes there is a feeling of sailing too close to the wind, a sort of, "Oh you can't say that, they'll be so cross!"' But she has learnt to rationalise and even exploit her anxieties, for she realises now that

> for everybody who will be angry about something or other there will be other people who will say, 'Ah, thank goodness someone has said that.' I try very hard not to feel intimidated by some sort of mysterious 'they' out there who will be angry with me – because they are not necessarily there at all and they don't necessarily have power.

Leslie Dick is more humorous. Her post-modernist first novel, *Without Falling*, grapples with the Angel in an intense and profane way, deliberately confronting many of feminism's sacred cows – masochism, guilt, the nature of subjectivity. It interrogates femininity, understanding it as a socially constructed trap that women are born into and then absorb, and it insists upon an understanding of that internalised structure: 'You can't just forbid.' Leslie Dick, from her position of serious irreverence, characterises the Angel as a 'critical feminist eye looking over the shoulder and going "tut-tut-tut" and going "What! His enormous penis! You can't write that!"' If the writer does not reject her, then she will be unable to write truthfully. Her work will be a sham, and it will probably also be self-righteous and irritating.

The Priest in the Closet

Down the centuries, artists have been frequently and often savagely critical of the establishment – biting the hand that feeds them, attacking the culture from which they were born. Unlike painting, music, film or theatre, writing has no public arena, but is the most private of arts. Some academics argue that the novel is the most naturally subversive form, because of the hidden nature of its medium, whose power resides precisely in its private and secret pleasures and its uniquely disruptive possibilities. Certainly, there are difficulties in writing from within the folds of the establishment, since much fiction thrives upon contradiction, opposition, even conflict, and is written against the rules of convention.

It is hardly surprising, then, that very few women write from the folds of official religion, which is beset with rules, and which has traditionally oppressed women (although, of course, pre-occupation with faith and spirituality, doubt, guilt and death, runs through literature). But while very few women write as established spokeswomen of their religion, several are marked by their diverse religious experience: Maya Angelou, Gloria Naylor, Toni Morrison, Mary Gordon, Sara Maitland, Mary Lavin, Leland Bardwell ... Some of these, particularly the black American writers, for whom religion means faith and politics and community and power, use their religious background as support and inspiration.

Others, particularly the Irish women writers, for whom religion means constraint and misogyny, struggle with its lingering and tenacious power over their lives. For them the Priest lurks within the Closet, spreading guilt, obsession, and a sense of loss. But Ireland is a country of peculiar contradictions for women, which were drawn out by Mary Dorcey. She said that while 'the dominance of the Catholic Church, especially in the areas of sexual morality and family law, makes it a very oppressive society for women', yet 'there is a bonding and sympathy between women that you might not find in a more "developed" country'. Also there is still not the claustrophobic emphasis upon romantic and exclusive relationships between men and women. And she insisted that in spite of the outward conformity, 'there is a special indulgence of the rebel and the eccentric'. Mary Dorcey is 'continually surprised' to find herself still in Ireland, explaining her rootedness by 'the intimacy, the ease of friendship, the intensity' of the country, and by the sense of language being so alive. The clear oppressions of Catholicism, which have been particularly strong for Mary Dorcey as a woman, a feminist, an atheist, a poet, a socialist and a lesbian, also make Ireland into an intense, fascinating and compelling country. Irish writers deal in diverse ways with religious faith, which has been tightly woven into the whole fabric of society.

Mary Lavin is one of the few Irish women who has not broken with her Catholic faith. She writes her finely observant short stories with an ease which still astonishes her – on buses, as her children and then grandchildren clamber over her, in an interregnum between two chores, at the kitchen table. She never wanted to be a writer ('I loved reading so much I couldn't imagine giving up the time to write') but now she says that the process of writing is so swift that it is like 'an arrow in flight – or better still, like a flash of forked lightning: all there on the sky at once, beginning, middle and end, because it traces its path so fast'.

She sees her Catholicism, like her Irishness, as a racial and environmental inheritance rather than a set of commandments and beliefs. And she is oddly dismissive of the power of Catholicism, insisting that it has no hold over her.

> The minute something happens in my Church that I don't like, I just write about it. I have never written anti-clerical stories; I have written stories about priests who have acted in ways that are shocking because their vocation is

supposed to be unselfish – but then I have only been
writing about them as men who happen to be priests.

This is a remarkably secular and apolitical view of Catholicism,
having little connection with faith, sin, guilt or even God. Rather
it is, like Ireland, a backdrop to individual people, whom Mary
Lavin believes are essentially the same wherever they live and
whatever they believe. Thus any disagreement she has with the
Church is individual and specific.

It is a large paradox that Mary Lavin appears to be so
constrained by the faith of her childhood. It is precisely because
she has been able to absorb her religion into her secular life,
taming its oppressions, that she has been able to stay within its
doors and still produce her layered and subtle stories. Other Irish
writers are more vehement, intense and personally exercised by
the faith they have thrown over.

Mary Dorcey points out that the Church considers 'that one
can never cease to be a Catholic, one can only "lapse"'. In her
case the 'taint' is a 'kind of metaphysical itch, a need to find
purpose beyond the everyday and material'. It is also the know-
ledge of guilt, the power of prayer, the difficulty of being female
and the sense of living in a vast and Godless world. Catherine
Brophy, who did not find her rejection of the Church painful,
nevertheless admits that it took her a long time to feel 'grand as
a woman and a sexual being'. The subject of her first novel,
The Liberation of Mary McCabe, charts the struggle towards
triumphant and spiritually charged atheism. Leland Bardwell
says that she is a 'Protestant atheist, as opposed to a Catholic one'.
She also pointed out the contradictions in being a woman writer
in Ireland who retained her faith: 'the struggle has been enormous
to reach any kind of liberal thinking – and if you are a writer you
must be aware of this, otherwise I don't see how you get
anything down at all'. She talks of a writer inhabiting 'the
imaginative spaces of her mind': if those spaces are cluttered with
commandments, with rules that oppress women, with doctrin-
aire notions of sin, with a strict sense of the hierarchy of things
(including the order which places woman below man), with

male authority figures (God, Pope, bishop, priest, father and husband), then it is 'difficult to see how a corner can be sufficiently cleared for the act of writing'.

Mary Dorcey, Catherine Brophy and Leland Bardwell are describing a rejection of dogma rather than belief. Their conversion to atheism denies misogyny, patriarchal authority and female imprisonment rather than belief itself. And their very denial of Catholicism structures and textures their writing. The rhythms of religious ritual and prayer, the pervading sense of guilt and death, the stink of hypocrisy, the emptiness of a Godless world, the helplessness of women trapped within a religious structure, are subjects for their work. That is equally true of Mary Gordon, the North American writer whose novels are pervaded by a sense of guilt, and often a catastrophic destiny. Mary Gordon's obsessive returns to the territories of faith, sin, doubt and a consciousness of duty give her writing a distinctive and compelling flavour. She is always portraying a world in which things are not what they seem – beneath the ordered surface of daily rituals and lucid prose another, more disturbing, reality lurks.

One of the few British women who writes not merely about, but through, Christianity is Sara Maitland. She describes the socially motivated Scottish Presbyterianism of her upbringing as 'community religion with a hint of noblesse oblige', which was 'unattractive, dour and intellectually unsound' and whose 'loss was no loss at all'. At Oxford, however, she was impressed by the Catholic Marxists she met, who were 'doing better than most left-wing people at keeping human relationships together', and in 1972 she became a Christian. 'I came to believe that Christianity was absolutely true and as absolutely true made absolute sense at a level that synchronised things in a way that nothing else did, except perhaps feminism.'

Being a feminist and a Christian is, she says, only a problem for some of her readers. For herself, the difficulties are 'practical rather than metaphysical' and the advantages enormous: the richness and referential possibilities of Christianity means that, as in life, it can 'synchronise' literature. She appreciates its huge image-structure ('if you are going to hold a novel together, it is very handy'). In *Virgin Territory*, for example, she has as her central concern and symbol an image that has been worked over by Christianity for 2,000 years – virginity. The resonances it has in theological, political, literary and feminist terms are self-proliferating and convoluted. Religion can be used in the same way as feminist writers often use myth or magic – as a deep pool of the familiar and strange into which the writer can dip.

Virgin Territory is an explicitly theological and sometimes polemical novel which explores the conflicts between faith and modernity, Christianity and feminism, will and desire. In Sara Maitland's short stories, however, religious faith gives wings to her prose. Rather than constraining them, it is a liberating force, feeding the imagination. *A Book of Spells* is about magic, witches, congruence, love, adolescent and adult dreams. It is witty, wry and emotional, full of weirdness and subjectivity. In her 'After-words' she describes her God as 'careless, random, extravagant, indiscriminate' and her faith as the

> continuous, inescapable sense of the power and the
> mystery and the danger and profligacy of it all. I mean *all*,
> from the bizarre goings-on inside each atom . . . right
> through to the social complexity of history and class and
> gender and race and individual experience.

For her, religious faith flashes glory over the smallest and largest things in life. The synchronising and illuminating power that religion has in Sara Maitland's writing is a useful reminder of how a belief (Christianity, feminism, socialism . . .) can flood a novel with meaning rather than stiffen it with ideology, and widen it with a sense of values rather than narrow it with inherited ethics.

Such transforming power of formal faith is found more often in the United States and Latin America, where Christianity is less of a Sunday affair, more of a realignment of values and perceptions. In North America the religious revival has its dark side: the Moral Majority that burns books and denounces freedoms in

91

the name of God and the service of Mammon; the reactionary and misogynist politics of many of the evangelists; the television Christianity that invades the lives and homes of the spiritually needy, preaching self-sacrifice and immediate redemption. But among black communities, religion takes on a dynamic and liberating role. It has a political and social meaning as well as an individual one; it can be subversive as well as spiritual. A number of black North American women writers have a strong religious belief, which permeates their fictions and which has nothing to do with dogmas. Rather, religion for writers such as Maya Angelou or Gloria Naylor is invigorating, politically validating and vital. Their faith, which encourages the sense of self-value and community pride, is a foundation for their bold writing, giving it a resilience and magical affirmation so lacking in British writing.

The Wolf at the Door

Despite the best literary and artistic traditions, it is not romantic to starve in a garret – and as Emma Tennant wryly observed, most people cannot even afford a garret nowadays. The image of writing by guttering candlelight in a cold bedsit, choosing to sacrifice the normal pleasures of life for the compulsions of writing, and working for love not money, is romantic nonsense. Writers have to pay the gas bill, clothe the child, fill the cupboard. The increased capital within the publishing business, and the dramatically increased wealth of a handful of writers, emphasises the feeling of relative poverty among most writers.

While the low amounts of money that writers earn is not precisely a form of market censorship, it does often mean that they have to write in corners of their day, relying on other sources of income. Shena Mackay has written nine wayward, eccentric and vigorous novels – all of which have been well-reviewed and found a respectable readership. She has never been paid more than £5,000 as an advance. If over the last twenty-five years she had relied solely on the money coming in from her chosen work, she would have been well below the poverty line.

As it is, she has had to do a series of part-time jobs, from reviewing books to picking mushrooms. Maureen Duffy has written numerous fine novels, and also several collections of poetry. She is now one of Britain's best-established writers – but all her life she has struggled financially, living in basements and one-bedroom flats. She was fifty before she could buy her first house. In 1988 a TV film was made of her novel *Gorsaga*, for the first time boosting her income above its meagre sufficiency. She resents the fact that writing is a 'middle-class occupation, and writers are expected to live in a middle-class way – but they don't earn middle-class wages', and she believes that they are 'constantly obstructed by the question, "How am I going to eat?"' Sara Maitland earned £9,994 in 1986 ('which really pissed me off') from writing-related activities. If she was solely responsible for her two children, she would have needed to have looked for other sources of income. Maggie Gee has done better than most women writers – but still if her total earnings were annualised they would be well below £10,000 a year (though boosted by the £25,000 advance paid for *Grace*). Alison Fell says that she has 'never had money and never expects to have any -- but I guess I am doing what I want to be doing'.

The lack of an assured income, and the often tiny sums paid out in royalties, have two possible effects on the writer's work. The first and most obvious is that she will not have large amounts of time and energy for writing. The second, and more difficult to assess, is that she may consciously try to write the kinds of books that might become 'bestsellers'.

Of course, at an obvious level it is only sane to try to write bestsellers – not only does every writer want to earn a decent living, she also wants to reach as wide a readership as possible. A novel that reaches only 300 people will not usually be that wonderful, nor does there seem much point in being a 'truthteller' to a handful of the already converted. But the tension for writers of producing the kind of novel they want, and producing one they know will sell, is often severe. At what point does selling become selling out?

The tension might be creative, as exemplified by Maggie Gee, who is clear about her anxiety. She poses the questions, 'What sort of writing is legitimate?' and 'Who are you actually writing for?', and links her anxiety to her socialism, explaining that 'there are problems about writing in certain kinds of ways that curtain off a lot of people. Literary novelists are an elitist category and are read by a small number of people; they get more media coverage than sales.' She admits that with her first novel, *Dying in Other Words*, it 'hadn't really crossed my mind that there might be a political problem with being an "experimental writer" – I used to think it was rather glamorous and now I think it is death'. She is increasingly bothered by the attitude that says, 'Serious literature is read and taught in universities.'

Speaking from the other side of the cultural divide between 'serious' and 'popular' authors, Sally Beauman reiterates Maggie Gee's concern: 'If you write a marvellous book and it is read by 2,000 to 3,000 people, most of whom are educated and middle-class, then I think you have a problem.' Would Dickens, she asks, be writing for *East Enders* if he were alive today?

Few writers would consider writing a *Destiny* – and anyway they probably could not; it takes a special kind of talent. But many worry about the implications of being 'serious'. Leslie Dick's optimistic and enthusiastic belief in readers' desire and ability to read difficult books, and her refusal to see the elitism of avant-garde writing as a problem, is rare. And Leland Bardwell's stricture – 'I would never write to a public because I thought it would sell; never never in any circumstances' – is unusually uncompromising and apparently self-destructive. Most writers recognise that they tread what Elaine Feinstein calls 'the tightrope between accessibility and some kind of integrity'.

A handful of writers do manage to straddle the popular and serious. Fay Weldon is an obvious example. Writing consistently biting, witty and irreverent books about contemporary society and morality, she is also one of Britain's entertainers. Her books have accessibility and their own integrity; they sell in tens of thousands; they are made into television films. She has even imitated Dickens in writing a serialised novel for *Woman* magazine, genuinely making up each episode that week. Moreover, she has become something of a social pundit, taking part in television debates, writing mocking and jocular articles in newspapers, becoming a spokeswoman for the writers. Fay Weldon has become her own industry, parodying and commenting upon herself; over-productive and sometimes over-praised; venomously critical but never quite a threat. She is an obvious example of the popular-serious writer only because there is little competition. And she can get away with moral intensity because she dresses it up in the sprightly, throwaway charm of her prose.

The Child at the Study Door

Motherhood brings the same fulfilment and difficulty for women writers as for any other women – except that women writers usually work from home. They are more vulnerable than most to the demanding or plaintive voice at the study door. The problem of devoting enough time to the child or children while being committed to work can seem irresolvable. Zoë Fairbairns has chosen not to be a mother, and while she says that her choice was made independently of her writing, yet she does not think that she could have shared out her devotions and organised her priorities.

When Joan Riley describes her typical day, as a single mother of two children who also works outside the home, then her output as a novelist emerges as an extraordinary act of energy and will.

> I get about five hours' sleep because I get to bed late and then have to get up really early if I'm going to get any real writing done. I'll rise at about 4.30 and write until the children get up. And I always give them four hours in the evening; that is important to me and them. Later, when they have gone to bed, I'll invariably have to give a talk or help someone with editing or something like that. So I can only work on my novels between 4.30 and when the children get up. I've got to write very quickly or it never

gets done. I do have a frenetic lifestyle and my energy comes in cycles. When the cycles peak I can do so much, but when they are low I still can't escape from all the things I've promised to do so I just have to grit my teeth and get through them. It is really hard.

But having children does not act as an obstacle to writing, so much as lend a different shape to the writing day, and to the writer's life, in a way that very few men can ever genuinely experience or appreciate. The Indian writer Anita Desai has 'made motherhood into a writerly virtue', fitting her writing around her children. And Sara Maitland dismisses the notion of writing mothers being any different from any other kind of working mother:

Nobody asks if having children puts you off being a bus conductor – if you feel you have to choose between having children and writing, well then, you have to choose; having the choice between being a writer and being a bus conductor, I'd rather be a writer. Having the choice between having children and not having them, I'd rather have children. Overall, I simply do what I do because I like it.

But many women emphasise the difference motherhood makes to their perceptions of the world, and therefore to their writing, rather than dwelling upon the financial imperatives and time pressures that come with childcare.

Shena Mackay loved being a mother. Although she has always struggled to support her children, she is grateful as a writer for the way that having them added an extra dimension to the eccentric and wayward visions of her novels.

They brought a sense of my own mortality. I was only twenty when the first of my three children was born and sometimes I am haunted by the thought that they might end up in a home and I won't be there to protect them.

The impact that mother love can have upon a writer is tragically exaggerated by Antonia Byatt's experience. She has three daughters, but always describes herself as having four children. At the age of eleven her only son ran out in front of a car and was killed. It took her the span of his life to feel that life could again be bearable, and his death led 'to a sort of nihilism'. She has described the long agony of bereavement in 'July's Ghost', a story in the collection *Sugar*. Here the pain is experienced at one remove – the tale of loss is narrated by the mother's lodger to a sympathetic stranger. The mother's agony is frantic and prolonged:

> After he died the best hope I had, it sounds silly, was that I would go mad enough so that instead of waiting for him every day to come home from school and rattle the letter box I might actually have the illlusion of seeing or hearing him come in. . . . They said, he is dead, and I thought cooly, *is* dead, that will go on and on till the end of time, it's a continuous present.

The long-ago loss and the fierce love has coloured her writing: death sits in all of her novels and she admits to being obsessed by it – 'it is like looking through the wrong end of a telescope'.

As Tillie Olsen pointed out in her short story 'As I Stand Here Ironing', women have found and will always find ways around practical obstacles – although, as she revealed in her book *Silences*, they will also suffer and be halted by them. Women will write at night or in the early hours of the morning. They will, like Mary Lavin, scribble paragraphs on the bus and pages as the children clamber over them. They will find small corners in an overcrowded day. Women who work and are mothers experience the simultaneous demands of the public and private world. They experience the relentless trivia and the huge significance of childcare. They learn to see large meanings in small events, and large events in closer perspective.

Feminism and feminist literature has not paid enough attention to the issues of motherhood. In the 1970s the emphasis was necessarily upon women's rights in the world outside the house: the right to work, to have equal pay, to be treated equivalently to men under the law – the right, almost, to escape from children as easily as men still can. And much fiction took up this angle of vision. In the *Children of Violence* series, Doris Lessing gives her protagonist, Martha Quest, the blunt choice between devotion to her daughter and individual survival. Martha literally flees her marriage, house, daughter and country in order to find her self.

Several years later, Marilyn French's *Her Mother's Daughter* attempts to show the awful tyranny of a mother's unconditional love for her children – but her relentless focus upon woman as parent neglects woman as careerist or sexual being, and her impenetrable gloom obscures all the positive aspects of bringing up children. Only now, with novels like Maggie Gee's *Grace* (written just after she had become a mother for the first time) and Toni Morrison's *Beloved*, are women beginning to combine the largeness and the trivia of childcare in their writings.

Fruitful anxiety

'No doubt I am prey to a good deal of self-censoring,' says Elizabeth Hardwick, Southern American writer and co-founder of *The New York Review of Books*, 'but I feel that often one doesn't have enough.' She is translating a term of inhibition into one of valuable self-criticism, of repression into discipline. 'Self-censorship can actually be the vital criticism of the creative act one is performing.' Elizabeth Hardwick writes slowly and painstakingly. She thinks that many novelists let words on to the page which should never be there; that many novels are needlessly sloppy, and should be subjected to severe and fastidious 'self-censorship' before they are ever submitted to a publisher. And according to her, writing blocks usually occur for a straightforward rather than glamorously convoluted and tortured reason: that the writer simply has nothing to say, and therefore should not try to say it.

Her dismissal of writers' anxieties is brisk and no-nonsense, but she has a fundamental point. The fear of self-censorship should be balanced by a fear of self-complacency. The question, 'What words and ideas of potential value am I not letting through?' can only be effective if it is countered by the alternative question, 'What am I letting through that would be better censored by my critical faculties?'

Elaine Feinstein points to another crucial difference: that between self-censorship and potentially fruitful anxiety. One is obstructive and the other constructive for a writer. She says that she has no ideologies to fetter the imagination – but she does have 'pieties'. Negotiating a way through these pieties is a hazardous business because 'if you don't approach them, you have nothing to say about what makes you most anxious – and yet I would feel profoundly uneasy if I seemed to be recommending courses of action that would appal me'. She cites as an example the anxieties posed in the novel she was writing when interviewed in 1988. She wanted to look at the ways in which the child–mother relationship is altered by the mother's newly independent position in the world.

> If you, the mother, become the prow pushing out into
> the sea, then what do the children think of as 'mother'? It
> is a matter of interest and bewilderment for me: if I think
> about the kind of woman I would like my sons to marry,
> then I realise at once I don't want some kind of
> self-seeking, pushing prow at all. So does that mean that I
> want a completely different sort of person to succeed than
> the one I want to be living with in the real part of my
> own life?

Elaine Feinstein's novels are preoccupied with what happened in Europe during the 1940s – this, she says, 'has warped my perception of the world, and has made it impossible for me to be utopian, even in the 1960s'. As a Jew, the discovery of the Holocaust shook her with a horror that she has never since been able to shrug off.

> I'm talking about how, when far too young, I discovered
> the absolutely extraordinary ruthlessness men and women

were able to show to other men, women and even
children. It was a terrible thing to discover – that people
could do these things has prevented me from ever again
believing in the goodness of men or women.

And the sense of horror haunts what she writes: it lies across her
depictions of guilt, individual and collective betrayals, love and
fidelity, how one person fits into his or her society. There is the
sense in her most successful works that, delicately but relent-
lessly, she is probing the sorest parts of her own, and our
collective, conscience.

The probings of Elaine Feinstein are relentless, but also tactful
and sensitive. They approach the pain or taboo of private
experience indirectly and cautiously, and so expose what blunter
approaches might simply callous over. The discriminatory
process of her writing obeys Elizabeth Hardwick's warning –
that self-censorship should be used as a 'vital criticism of the
creative act one is performing'. And many women writers have
subjects about which they find it difficult but imperative to write.
Maggie Gee spoke of her difficulty in writing about cruelty to
children. Antonia Byatt talked about her painful compulsion to
write about death and bereavement. Sue Miller found describing
the sexual act explicitly and yet erotically extremely difficult –
which is probably why the sexual passages in *The Good Mother*
are so successful.

But Elizabeth Hardwick's warning is ignored by many
women writers of the 1980s. The Kathy Acker school of writing
has little time for self-restraint, preferring a kind of literary
freedom in which anything is permissible. The painfully acquired
'pieties' of which Elaine Feinstein talked are the bourgeois
inhibitions and genteel euphemisms that Acker so crudely attacks
in her writing. Fruitful anxiety is not a notion to which she would
be attracted.

Kathy Acker is an American writer who now lives and works
in London. Both in the United States and in Britain her work and
her well-marketed self have received a good deal of media
attention. Kathy Acker likes to shock. The way that she dresses,

talks and writes is deliberately outrageous. She does not just break taboos, she drops them from a great height and with a great deal of noise and glee. Sado-masochism, group sex, extreme male brutality, incest and child abuse are described in graphic, even pornographic, detail. Exaggerated post-modernism is combined with studied post-feminism: meaning is never absolute, but always constructed, shifting and subjective; beliefs and desires are never sacrosanct, but always to be violently ruptured. Virtue is the only dirty word in her novels.

Novels like Kathy Acker's *Blood and Guts in Highschool*, *Don Quixote* and *Empires of the Senseless* have enjoyed a kind of cult status in the last years of the 1980s, heralded as the post-feminist equivalent of works by Burroughs or Henry Miller. In them, amorality becomes a kind of despairing morality, and apolitical irreverence is the only sincere form of politics. Like the infamous and abused bricks in the Tate Gallery, the first neo-everything Acker-type novel might possess the power initially to shock the reader into reappraisal. It may expose hypocrisy and shake sentimentality, leading the reader to question attitudes to sexuality and language. But the second is monotonous, and the third infantile. The politics of derision are slack and trendy; their linguistic renderings lack craft and care. Such writing flaunts the pieties and indirections that Elizabeth Hardwick urges and Elaine Feinstein and others practise. It suffers and grows tediously vacuous from its uninhibited contempt.

A modernist writer who, unlike Acker, does succeed in portraying disturbing female fantasies and perverse male ones with power, intelligence and precision is Jenny Diski. Her first novel, *Nothing Natural*, is an impressive debut revealing hidden and destructive drives and desires in a chilling prose. Her second novel, *Rainforest*, again takes up the question of 'naturalness' and 'man's place in Nature', placing chaos and order in opposition, and demonstrating how irrational sexual desires can break through the fences of well-adjusted behaviour, to produce confusion, rage and crisis. Diski is at her strongest when she writes of obsessive sexual relationships, of emotions that border on fetishes, and desires that can become pornographic. Explicit and often disturbing in her descriptions, she is a serious rather than gimmicky breaker of literary and female taboos.

At the opposite end of the linguistic and political spectrum to Kathy Acker stand writers such as Antonia Byatt, whose sense of restraint and painful extraction of meaning from experience is a grave contrast to Acker's facility. In Byatt's writing we see how self-censorship and self-discipline can become the transforming filters through which experience is refracted. She does not shy away from the subjects over which Acker makes loud rude noises. Rather, she brings the weight of her emotion and intellect to bear upon them.

Antonia Byatt's writing make the perilous and subtle nature of moral urgency coherent and painful. Her writing is clear, fervently lucid, not afraid of extremes nor of paradoxes. We all know that extremes exist – but we rely on their inarticulacy to keep them muted and bearable. Byatt, however, brings a monumental clarity to bear upon the minds and emotions of her characters. Throughout her novels, and carried over into her collection of muscular stories, *Sugar*, is the insistence upon the physical and mental hurts that coalesce into experience; the collision of culture with the individual; the connections between an individual, a culture and a nation. In Antonia Byatt's painfully elucidated novels, reading a poem can be as erotic as having an orgasm; riding a bicycle as mentally reflective as pondering on history. She reaches, in the most successful of her writing, the satisfying and painful state in which emotions are intellectual and the intellect profoundly emotional.

Antonia Byatt deals with the forbidden and anxious areas of her consciousness in a cruelly unblinking and yet tactful fashion. There is a constant and compelling disjuncture between the violent extremes that she describes and the grave language she employs. The tightrope is meaning: using the pure integrity of language to span the violent extremities of physical life, and the ingrowing nuances of mental reflection. And the task she sets herself – to preserve language, 'keeping it as flexible and large as possible' – is her way of safeguarding meaning, for she believes that culture resides within language and will be eroded with it.

Concerned with meaning, Antonia Byatt has no easy template to lay over her characters and their lives. Her morality lies precisely and finely within the difficulty, fragility and painfulness of extracting meaning from experience.

Such a formal and linguistic definition of the writer's task may seem far removed from the social and political urgencies of many women writers. But it too insists, in its own way, that words can make things happen. Language is an instrument of power and of cultural survival.

Writing against oppression: writing as survival

Black North American writers offer us a devastating account of how this survival, in Byatt's case metaphorical, can become literal. They have written, talked, preached, sung and taught, as it were, for their very lives. Language has kept their culture alive. Their writing also brings us uncomfortably close to the bleak theory that much of the most affecting art often wells up from under the greatest repression; that language becomes most powerful and imaginatively free when it is the single freedom left. The caged bird (giving her the title to the first of her series of autobiographies, *I Know Why the Caged Bird Sings*) becomes Maya Angelou's symbol of the power of language, and the willed affirmation among people who are otherwise deprived of power. The caged bird – the black woman with an ancestry of slavery and a present of oppression – pours out her soul in a joyful act of defiance and survival.

Maya Angelou in her resilient and idiosyncratic account of one life, Alice Walker in her fictional and factual evocations of black women's rich and painful lives, Toni Morrison in her fierce and emotional novels which explore the black woman's history and present, all highlight a startling contrast: American black women have written passionate, rich, audacious novels, full of what Alice Walker calls 'dangerous possibility', whose defiant optimism finds few equivalents in white British or North American writing.

The theory that art often is actually enhanced by forms of

oppression might seem to be borne out by the experience of the New Zealand writer Janet Frame, who, like some black women writers in the United States, invests her language with new and shocking meaning. Her writing literally saved her from extinction. Born into a poor New Zealand railway family, acutely shy as a child, she spent eight of her first ten years of adulthood in the back wards of mental hospitals, struggling to defend her frail sense of self against the idiotic diagnoses of the psychiatric profession. There by accident – 'a sane person caught unwillingly in the revolving doors of insanity' – she managed eventually to escape, also through an accident. Condemned 'like a slum dwelling' to a lobotomy, she survived only because one doctor stumbled across the fact that she was a budding writer.

Frame's descriptions of her experience, recorded in her second volume of autobiography, *An Angel At My Table*, and fictionalised in *Faces in the Water*, are appalling but eventually exhilarating. She describes how, trapped among 'the raging mass of people' and 'the immovable debris of sickness', she learnt a new 'mad language, which created with words, without using reason, has a new shape of reason'. And in spite of the prolonged nightmare of the experience, Janet Frame is fiercely grateful for the benefits it brought to her as a writer, insisting that the 'territories of loneliness' resemble the land between life and death and

> bring inevitably a unique point of view that is a
> nightmare, a treasure and a lifelong possession; at times I
> think it must be the best view in the world, ranging even
> further than the view from the mountains of love, equal
> in its rapture and its chilling exposure.

Janet Frame survived because she was a writer – and she became a writer of unusual power because she has suffered the death-in-life of incarceration. The experience of madness and squalid teeming confinement actually brought her closer to an imaginative freedom.

The extreme barriers that face some writers may shape their

writing in particular and poignant ways. But indifference or direct oppression still cannot be said to be 'good' for literature. The difficulties of combining motherhood with writing, the endemic prejudices against women, the financial insecurity of women in a back-to-the-home climate are discriminating frosts. Censorship and self-censorship can nip a work of art in the bud. As William Blake wrote, 'And if a blight kill not a tree and it still bear fruit, let none say that the fruit was in consequence of the blight.'

five

THE FEMINIST NOVEL AND THE SMALL WORLD OF REALISM

The most triumphantly feminist literature of the last decade is that which has been occupied rather than preoccupied by feminism; shaped and permeated by a feminist consciousness, rather than trapped within an inherited feminist structure. But it seems that the tag 'feminist' is now often used to describe a *bad* feminist book. Just as we think of Dostoevsky's *Crime and Punishment* as transcending the crime novel rather than using its characteristics and structure to the greatest possible effect, or we think of *Villette* as a great novel rather than a great ghost story, so we tend to erase 'feminist' from the most successful feminist novels, leaving it as an implicit and rather bizarre criticism of the rest.

That may be why so many women writers, who welcome the adjective 'feminist' for their personal lives, react with a kind of horror at the suggestion that they actually write 'feminist novels'. Emma Tennant shies away from the label because 'nothing dates faster than ideologically committed literature'. Maggie Gee insists that she is not a feminist writer because

> I don't think I've ever been ideologically correct; I couldn't be – it is just true that it is more central to me to be a writer than to be a feminist. Writing is the point of my life and feminism comes later; when I am writing it comes from levels of myself that are not politically conscious.

Elaine Feinstein urges that 'you have to understand that in the sense of being ideologically sound, I am not a feminist, that kind of thing makes me anxious'. Antonia Byatt expresses anxiety at a '1970s type of feminism which tells me I should be preoccupied with the smallness of women's lives.'

Writer after writer makes an explicit separation between being a feminist and being a feminist author – until it comes as a great relief to come across Angela Carter describing herself as 'a feminist writer because I'm a feminist in everything else and one can't compartmentalise these things in one's life'. Or across Mary Dorcey's insistence that she would not feel so uneasy with the terms 'feminist', 'Irish', or 'lesbian' writer if cover blurbs also made such proclamations as 'distinguished white male middle-class heterosexual gives us poems that speak from his condition'. As she says, 'No ideas can be free of our class and racial background, but we have different voices and a common history.'

It is as if the description 'feminist writer' were an accusation. Those writers who reject the term all seem to have in mind some kind of stereotypical feminist novel: angst-ridden, preoccupied with individual and often autobiographical suffering, 'brave', navel-gazing, politically obvious and unsubtle. The list continues, with the obvious devices – the therapist's couch as an introduction to past pain, the literal journey back into the geography of growing up, which is also a journey towards self-knowledge, the discovery and overuse of the cliché that 'the personal is the political' – and with recurring and savagely felt preoccupations. The stereotype does not actually exist: it is a composite version of numerous mediocre feminist novels. Writers who are feminists tend not to defend themselves against the charge of introverted domestic realism perfected by someone like Anita Brookner, or the *Spectator*-ish novel of manners by someone like Jane Ellison, although such novels are just as numerous and can be just as stereotypically bad. But the bad feminist novel is often what they most fear from themselves: self-exposing, self-indulgent or self-concerned.

The stereotypical 'feminist novel' has as its model a small-scale domestic realism, whose traditional and familiar structure is manipulated, and injected with a moralising feminist conscious- ness. Sara Maitland points out that this form of feminist literature also has links with the realist romance – only instead of the heroine finding her hero and galloping off with him on a white charger, now she finds either her perfect female partner, or, more commonly, her long-sought-after independence. But the reliance of the realist novel upon the small and self-contained worlds of usually middle-class individuals can seem trivial and self- indulgent. Perhaps it should no longer serve as the most domi- nant and well-used model for feminist writers.

Realism's small worlds

In America and Britain, from authors and editors, there has been a consistent and urgent demand to leave domestic realism behind, and move towards something less insular.

In an age where the concerns of the planet encroach upon the provincial, where self-preservation collides with anxiety about the outside world, and where materialism prospers at the cost of spiritual or emotional richness, many writers feel the need to be truth-tellers in a wide and moral sense. The contemporary domestic novel frequently cannot bear the burden of its writer's preoccupations. Few realistic novels of the 1980s have had the weight and gravity of their ancestors. They have failed to hook into the larger world in a way which merges domestic realism with larger preoccupations. It would be difficult to write an 1980s version of *Middlemarch*. Rather, they often construct and occupy sealed-off worlds, and are uninvaded by the national fears and international anxieties of the late twentieth century.

Antonia Byatt considers that perhaps although we have not quite come to the end of nineteenth-century realism as a possible model, yet the English novel, the small novel about class and the home, is finished simply because 'there have been too many of them – nobody except the English are interested in this small form'. Her own admired models are realists: Balzac 'because his people do everything; they have sex lives and social lives and political lives and lives on a huge world scale'; George Eliot because 'she knows exactly how people behave and she likes *things*, but then she also thinks about their context and attaches them'; and Proust. The 'attaching' that Antonia Byatt recognises in George Eliot, and the 'world scale' that she responds to in Balzac, are the missing elements in today's English realist novel.

Probably the best-known and most popular exponent of 'domestic realism' in Britain at the moment is Anita Brookner, who has steadily been turning out novels about the plight of the plain young woman with passions hidden beneath beautifully appropriate behaviour. Only with the surprise win of the 1984 Booker Prize did she become a household name; not only *Hotel du Lac* but all her previous novels, which up until then had had respectable but modest sales, became sudden bestsellers.

While the award of the Booker to *Hotel du Lac* raised a storm of protest in some quarters, it was also a popular choice for a book which became enormously popular itself. *Hotel du Lac* is slight and exquisite. It describes in immaculate detail the anatomy of the human heart and has no pretensions to world-scale grandness. Sober, ironic and restrained, it is everything that the flamboyant and extravagant *Nights at the Circus*, which that year was not even shortlisted, is not.

Hotel du Lac is a love story that catches at the hearts of anyone who has suffered in silence from unrequited passion. Its morality is mildly pessimistic. Eschewing heroines and villains and the grand gesture, it insists that good manners, hard work, endurance, class, culture and correct grammar are all-important. Edith Hope, the romantic novelist who, under her ironic manners, dreams of a romance that will fire her life, and the motley assortment of characters at the little hotel where she is staying, are all admonished by the author for their extravagances.

Brookner is attracted to the victim. Most of her heroines are women who want nothing so much as domestic bliss, and are living in the wrong age, unequipped to deal with its unwritten rules of conduct and unaided by a complacent feminism which ignores the fates of wistful, plain and middle-class women like

Edith Hope. In *Misalliance* the central character, Blanche Vernon, is a woman of seemly behaviour who, when deserted by her husband for one of 'life's predators', pours all her energy into filling her days and behaving well. She is a self-confessed 'old-fashioned woman' wanting 'old-fashioned pleasures' – hearing the husband's step on the stair every evening; cooking well-balanced meals for two; sharing a view and a joke. In contrast to her modest demands and attractive reserve stands the 'modern', independent woman, the predator whom Brookner implies is actually 'indifferent to good'. Again, in *A Friend from England*, the debate between passion and duty is made into a dialogue between two contrasting women – liberated Rachel, and Heather, who opts for romantic love. Rachel, representative 'feminist' – even in the novel the word is placed within quotation marks, giving it an ambivalent edge – achieves independence by being withdrawn, cool, unengaged with the world. Her apparent strength emerges as a rather pitiable refusal to let her guard down. She is painfully dissatisfied with her liberated life. Such a definition of feminism is implicit in all of Anita Brookner's novels: harsh, cold, complacent and hostile to a great number of silently unhappy women. Feminism, it is implied, is a dogmatic creed that disguises a predatory impulse or a dissatisfaction that is hidden and sublimated.

Yet Anita Brookner raises crucial questions, and it is not good enough for feminists simply to dismiss her writing. She conveys a sense that life is hostile to happiness, that women are separate beings who have been abandoned by men and by time, that feminism has often betrayed them, that 'something has gone wrong'. That strikes a chord with many women in the 1980s. It is a commonly heard and deeply felt complaint. The women's movement has often disregarded the emotions, anxieties and desires of an inarticulate majority. And one of the most dominant and powerful desires that many women have, sometimes against their own desire and will, is for security, romantic love and domestic fulfilment. Brookner captures the pain of women who have romantic dreams and drab lives; who, longing for male affection and the safety of dependency, live bravely independent

110

lives and suffer. It is futile to say that their desires are mistaken, that they should discover the delights of being single. Blanche Vernon in *Misalliance* turns to good works and art galleries to fill her days; she 'copes' with being alone – but her profound and abiding desire is to be the best beloved within a strictly traditional relationship.

Anita Brookner's plangent and wistful evocation of a world full of brave, silent and enduring women, betrayed by their dreams and abandoned by love, suggests a passive resignation. Much of the appeal of her novels – their beautiful sadness, their grave and formal intelligence, their scrupulous reserve – lies in a kind of surrender to the world's unfairness: 'This is how life is.' Her female characters acquire a dignity and low-key heroism by accepting, with irony and dignity and silence, their fates; not to be loved, not to be successful, not to be fulfilled or happy, not to be beautiful.

It is striking that Brookner's most fulsome reviewers are men. It is men who compare her with Jane Austen, neglecting the radical and subversive aspects of Austen's works for her 'little bit of ivory' charm. It is men who most admire the wit and beauty of Brookner's prose, and the access she has into the workings of the female heart. They also respond, perhaps unconsciously, to her melancholy perspective on woman's position in the world.

The feminist confessional

Realism was important to women writers and readers in the 1960s and 1970s. We needed novels to 'tell it like it is', showing the way that women lived, exploring personal and sharply contemporary issues. The books that Doris Lessing, Margaret Drabble, Iris Murdoch, Marge Piercy or Marilyn French wrote during those decades made a tremendous impact upon their readers. For the first time, women's experiences were treated as central and significant: it mattered that daily and domestic details were recorded; that shopping and cooking, nappies and sleepless nights, menstruation and sexual desire, heterosexual and homosexual relationships were written about from a woman's point of view. The stuff of female life was rendered in often illuminating detail. As Marilyn French points out, such a detailed and personal evocation meant that women no longer felt isolated within their own domestic situations; they had the impulse to change their lives. Fictional women sitting at kitchen tables drinking peppermint tea and discussing their problems is not a mundane literary event if real women see through that conversation a commentary on their own lives.

Confessions were not only good for the soul, but for the women's movement, for they swelled the wave of feminist self-awareness. The flood of feminist novels that were all in some way or other about female suffering in a patriarchal world (sexual abuse, inequality, rape, pregnancy and abortion, the trap of motherhood and female conditioning) often possessed literary as well as emotional value.

But while many of the more imaginative and original writers have moved to other forms, there is still a plethora of feminist confessionals. After two decades of feminism, it is surprising and disappointing that we have often gone no further than brave novels about individual suffering. After the anger and self-exposure and the translation of the personal into the political, feminism seemed poised to produce many more novels that look beyond individual suffering and healing. A continual and over-simplified accusation often hurled against the women's movement is that of navel-gazing and speaking in dogmas that no longer have any relevance – talking about whether we should shave our legs, whether we should wear pin-stripe suits to work, discussing feminism in middle-class, white and self-indulgent terms. And the same accusation could be made about some feminist literature. While there are women who are now writing in new and ambitious ways, the main body of feminist novels remain stuck in the literary traditions of the recent past or in a decontextualised and ahistoric present. The confessional novel, the brash contemporaneity of the Brat Pack novels, the cleverness of the minimalist novel, seem to reflect an age that lacks a rich sense of culture or a clear political awareness.

That does not mean that, taken individually, each of these lesser-known novels are no good. Many deserve to be more widely read than they actually are. But the tone set by this largely unreviewed and unnoticed mass whose sales are modest and shelf life short is a stale one of self-indulgence – what Sara Maitland calls 'little-heartedness'. And too often ideological correctness can take the place of genuine political anger or emotion.

Take two books published by The Women's Press in 1986, both of which are almost stereotypes of this feminist tradition. *Peeling*, by the Australian Grace Bartram, tells the story of Ally, who is abandoned by her husband after thirty years of marriage. The novel opens as Rowley announces he is leaving Ally, who hasn't changed her hairstyle, the colour of her lipstick or the nature of her views and expectations since their marriage. It is a well-managed scene, with Ally's red-hot rage releasing her as it has not done since adolescence. But the stage is a little too carefully set for her predictable rebirth into a liberated and political woman of the 1980s. She worries that she has not shaved her legs and that her daughter is a lesbian; she demonstrates her low expectations. Ally is in a cocoon, and the remainder of the novel is a process of peeling away the layers of her sedate and deeply conventional existence to discover an unexpected self. *Peeling* is a feminist novel of awakening which, unusually, has at its centre an older woman. But it is also a novel bound by feminist restrictions. There is a sense of over-inclusiveness – the desire to say everything, in one medium-length novel, about repression and possible transformation.

Such over-inclusion is the charge that lesbian-feminist writer Barbara Wilson levels against many of the lesbian feminist novels of the 1980s. Because 'many of us are trying to describe the kinds of lives we are leading at the moment, and that is hard to do, it tends to get ideological'. We want our characters to be 'correct'. There are some lesbian novels, she says, which suffer from the 'one of everything' syndrome – and she specifically cites another book published by The Women's Press, *Three Ply Yarn* by Caeia March. Caeia March's ambitious rendering of three women's voices, that are woven together into the novel's 'yarn', is a welcome breaking of the publishing silence about working-class lesbian experience. But the novel is overloaded with feminist dogma and stifled by its own propaganda. It never takes on a life of its own. Moreover, Caeia March slips into a particular kind of banality, making metaphors literal. At the end of the novel the characters' discovery that their mothers and grandmothers before them were also lesbians is an oversimplified and embarrassing re-working of feminist rediscovery and reclamation of history.

Both *Three Ply Yarn* and *Peeling*, for all their divergent perspectives (one lesbian, working-class and British; the other heterosexual and Australian), conform to the conventions of a particular kind of feminist realist novel. They are both brave and slightly worthy; they both explore the nature and causes of female suffering; and they both work through a series of obstacles towards an individual happiness of independence and self-awareness. Above all, though published in the 1980s they both have the musty smell of the 1970s – 'novels for our time' written at the wrong time – which gives their evident sincerity an unfortunate air of platitudinous earnestness.

Feminism successfully and effectively took up the realist literary model in the 1950s, 1960s and 1970s. Those were generations in which, it seemed, realism was an appropriate form for current preoccupations, and the novels of social realism had a great and enduring impact upon their readers. Many of the women writers of stature turned to realism, where they established their stature and moral urgency: Marge Piercy and Marilyn French; Iris Murdoch, Doris Lessing, and Margaret Drabble; Elaine Feinstein, Maureen Duffy and Antonia Byatt. But an extraordinary number of women are now turning from realism towards different, invented, forms.

There is also a movement by younger feminist writers away from the familiar and comforting form of realism. They are increasingly using and subverting other genres, more usually associated with light-hearted entertainment than with social preoccupations. Detective fiction and science fiction, romances, blockbusters and family sagas, thrillers and horrors are all being taken up by feminist publishers and feminist writers, eagerly read by women readers, and are being heralded by some as the way out of a literary cul-de-sac.

six

FEMINIST GENRES

The movement towards categorising works of fiction in order to package and market them more appealingly has been one of the major changes in the publishing world over the last two decades.

At first glance it appears that there has been a sudden proliferation in feminist genre writing: more science fiction and detective fiction, more romance and horror. In fact, books have been obsessively labelled. Readers are alerted: they are told where to go for their favourite type of novel, even if they are sometimes taken aback by the book that they pluck from the library shelf marked 'crime' or 'science fiction'. It is a trend, beginning in the United States and rapidly imported to Britain, of which all writers must be aware. Maureen Duffy, who has written a spy novel, a historical novel and a futurist novel, understands but regrets the need for labels, saying that she 'needs to find a place within literature for all the various genres'. Emma Tennant wryly admits that it is 'not surprising that I don't sell that well – I have always crossed genres and that makes me difficult to categorise'.

While the world 'genre' is often used to diminish a book, genre categories can be applied to every novel. Realism is just as much of a category as spy or western. The tag categorises the book and flags down the reader. It has been a remarkably successful marketing ploy. The boom in 'books for young adults', for example, relies upon defining a group of readers who previously have been ignored, and targetting them. It does not necessarily mean publishing new books, or books written specifically for a younger market. Teenagers are an increasingly powerful consumer group: advertisements are aimed at them, fashions specifically geared to them and magazines and even newspapers produced for them. Belatedly, many publishers now have a young adult list. It is not a radical development in literature but in marketing strategy.

The same principle largely applies to the increase in genre publishing. The advantages and disadvantages pull against each other. A genre is recognised (or created), defined and packaged – clearly helping the retailer by acting as a flag to the reader. If they like one novel in a particular series they can confidently go back for more; the appeal of a label may introduce them to books they would not otherwise open and to ideas they would not otherwise consider. But while the strategy can set standards, it also runs the danger of sinking literature into the porridge of standardisation, carrying the homogenising process of the writing programmes one stage further. Virago's first years are a shining example of the benefit of series to the reader; their classic reprints brought many readers to women's writing and to feminism. But Virago's more recent publications also signal the danger of series; many of their subsequent reprints have been mediocre, dutifully limping into the lists after their brighter sisters. That Virago have recognised the cul-de-sac of their once-successful packaging is evident in their redesigned jackets. The once-ubiquitous dark green has been supplemented first by 'avocado' green, and then by a chic modern illustration, retaining only the logo of the bitten apple. They need to break the stranglehold of their cultivated image. Books can become, as New York editor Kathy Anderson commented, 'derivative of themselves'.

And Virago was a forerunner in an uncharted terrain, into which other publishers soon hurtled. It has become overcrowded. The risk of jostling for space and readers is not that various series overlap – that might be all to the good – but that they become bland: a series for a series's sake, launched for its marketing appeal rather than its substance. It can bring about a peculiar reversal in publishing priorities – no longer, 'These are the books, how shall we package them?' but, 'This is the package, what books shall we insert?' Not, 'We have ten good science fiction novels, therefore we shall publish ten' but, 'We shall publish ten science fiction novels, therefore we have to find ten.' Series, even those with promising beginnings (as with the trendy Vintage Contemporary list in the United States) can become gimmicks, nice packages concealing emptiness. They can also become tyrannies, channelling literature into grooves.

Feminism and genres

Genre publishing attempts to popularise literature through labelling. It creates, and then cashes in on trends. It becomes like the clothes industry, forever marketing the latest fashion, unable to stand still and consolidate. The publishers of feminist books, threatened by changes in the industry, poached by bigger companies and no longer rooted in the old certainties of women's liberation, are forced on to the front line of change. They continually have to introduce and popularise in order to survive. The great virtue of their enforced innovations is that women's presses are forever one step ahead; they have been pioneers in important literary advances, bringing Arab writers, black American writers, third-world writers, homosexual writers and working-class writers to the insular publishing scene. Their great weakness is that they tend to over-produce, and overstrain innovation.

The questions raised by the process of popularisation are grappled with by feminism as a whole. Does it bring with it a welcome and rich diversity of feminist thought and expression, or dilute the power and urgency of feminist concerns? Does much-needed accessibility slither towards compromise, or blunt the cutting edge of theory? Has the increased consciousness of image, and of the importance of making feminist ideas attractive to those who have shied away from the word, given a new generosity and elasticity to feminism? Have the dramatic and

118

vital truths of feminism withered under the bright surface of images and design?

Such questions do not signal a harsh opposition (that feminism is either healthier or more debilitated in a commercial and image-conscious climate) so much as a paradox. For it appears that the women's movement, women's publishing and women's writing are both healthier and weaker; more popular and accessible, less powerful and transformative. And feminist writing, in responding to the wishes of its potential consumers, is both more secure because rooted in commercial success, and less confident because the soil of its first flowering has suffered erosion. The veritable flood of genres within the feminist presses – crime series, science fiction series, teenage fiction series, modern classic series, travel book series – testify to the new feminist spirit of inclusion, the infiltration of feminism into the mainstream and conversely, of the mainstream into the opened-out world of feminist publishing. They signal the freeing of women's writing from old shackles of puritanism (now feminism, as Leslie Dick put it, can be everything: 'easy, difficult, serious, fun, one hundred things at once') and at the same time confine writers to strict categories.

But while the boom in popular feminist series might be a response to a new, anti-puritanical spirit within feminism itself, it does not really herald a development within feminist literature. To take what had often been thought of as male genres, to find exciting new ways of invigorating old forms, is to inject the familiar with feminist consciousness. It is not, however, an intellectual progression. The proliferation of series, and the emphasis upon marketing and design, marks where we are – at a stage of consolidation, clarification and popularisation – rather than where we are going. They may reflect the present, but do not usually illuminate the future.

This raises a troubling, if well-worn, question: can a novel that is popular entertainment and is therefore confined by intrinsically conservative rules be converted to radical ends? And if not, does that imply that radical ideas are the preserve of the elite, only to be diluted down into accessibility? The boom in the study of popular culture, with academics analysing and sociologising the detective novel, soap opera or blockbuster into respectability, is a sign of left-wing puzzlement. How should we democratise culture without emptying it of political content; how recognise the transforming power of culture within mass entertainment? But the study of popular culture seems riven with its own ironies. It is a way for the middle-class and intellectual elite to explain to itself, often in an intellectually obfuscating way, the appeal of a culture which at first glance is politically at odds with its own. Feminist papers discuss, with footnotes, the racist yet seductive melodrama of *Gone With The Wind*, the troubling appeal of *Dallas*, or the regressive yet reassuring fantasies of Mills & Boon romances.

For we are presented with a fraught paradox: when feminist writers desert the high ground of 'serious' literature for the easier terrain of the more popular forms, they are being more political, in that they are rejecting the elitism of 'serious' writing, and yet they are no longer at the cutting edge of literature and its ideas.

Post-modernism in feminist hands

Post-modernism is one of those words that we use in a vague and baffled way, only battening down its meaning by context. Like realism but unlike most familiar genres, it is not *about* anything.

The language and examples of post-modernism can be most conveniently traced through architecture. Here, the movement emerges from the cute, rococo, mock-classic and neo-Georgian as one of parody, pastiche and obsession with the second-hand, fitting easily and blandly into a world where conservation has become the rage (the pubs with Victorian fittings, a neo-Georgian residence for Mrs Thatcher, the anodyne romantic revival illustrated by one strand of fashion and much of TV's advertising). In such a context, post-modernism, with its over-developed irony, its fear of commitment and of culturally distinct and unreferential forms, seems to identify with reaction and reflect a throwaway, trivialised world. It exemplifies a retreat from avant-garde radicalism into a facile and spurious nostalgia that parallels Mrs Thatcher's evocation of the Victorian era or Reagan's Wild West manner.

But post-modernism can also be seen in a progressive light, particularly when it is not traced through architectural examples but looked at in other art forms. Post-modernism in literature can appear as a form of liberation, a fragmented movement in which cultural plurality and ideological contradictions co-mingle. Such a synthesis of fragments seems especially promising when applied to feminism, which welcomes plurality and diversity.

Leslie Dick's first novel, *Without Falling*, was published in 1987 after many months of polite, and not-so-polite, rejection letters from publishers obviously baffled by a feminist psychoanalytical post-modernist novel about the language of masochism and desire. She wanted to 'write against the grain of romance, against the coherent identity of the strong woman, the feminist heroine, against various writerly strategies, against a story that has a beginning and middle and end'. Psychoanalysis and post-modernism are 'useful methods to try and interrogate, or question, or push up against, femininity'. Her comments on the nature of 1980s feminism echoed her comments on linguistic strategies. 'The most wonderful strength of feminism is and always has been its diversity and its heterogeneity.'

Without Falling, whose abrupt poetry and sudden disjunctures map our post-modern fractured world, was finally published by the newly launched Serpent's Tail, partly because of Leslie Dick's friendship with Kathy Acker. Kathy Acker's violent, parodic novels (many are ripped-off from classic texts, such as *Great Expectations* and *Don Quixote*) highlight the difficulties and possibilities of feminist post-modernism. In *Great Expectations* Acker re-writes Dickens (her novel opens 'Red everywhere'), Keats's *The Eve of St Agnes* (his sensuousness is over-ripened, and the poem's voyeurism and invasiveness become a form of rape in which the woman is literally an edible object), Victoria Holt and Proust. Texts we have inherited alive are returned to us blown and rotten. The safe ground of literature's past erupts, and all our expectations are wrenched into ugly shapes. Acker dwells upon degradation, patriarchal cruelty, macho language and extreme violations and obscenities in order to comment effectively upon our post-modern world. But at the same time she enacts and parodies that violation and obscenity, throwing up the same doubts as Andrea Dworkin in her venomous, obsessive attacks upon our pornographic world. How far can a feminist writer go in revealing the wrongs of a constructed society before she succumbs to it? Obscenities are simultaneously exposed and reproduced. The freedom of post-modernism can also be its lack of commitment to any form of belief. An attack upon coherent identities can also be an attack on a firm political position.

On the one hand, post-modernism is a reappraisal, undoing old meanings, illuminating the way that we live. On the other, it is a retreat from radicalism into the uncommitted and self-referential realm of parody and pastiche. Writers can use it in either way – or in both. A writer like Leslie Dick successfully manipulates its difficulties and parodies, but Kathy Acker converts them into degenerative anti-conventions. Like most genres, however, it is not inherently liberating. As Leslie Dick says, it is a 'tool' to be used or discarded in the creation of the 'mad million flowers blossoming'.

Detective novels

Crime writing is a perfect example of how the feminist consciousness can infiltrate and invigorate a familiar and much-loved form, but also of how feminism itself is challenged in the process.

Detective novels generally uphold conservative social values. However subverted, the form of a detective novel is neatly contained in closure – which is what makes them so satisfying to the reader. Order is disrupted by a crime, the wrongdoer is tracked down through clues, is exposed and judged (often in an amateur court where the suspects may be gathered as witness) – and punished. The traditional values which have been threatened are maintained, and they are emphasised by the small, stable, hierarchical and class-conscious worlds in which the crime often takes place – the school, nursing home, college or rural village. Those worlds are interconnected, often claustrophobic: wrong-doing explodes into them like an unguided missile, affecting every inhabitant and dragging in its wake the fear of anarchy. The detective novel, however, represents the very opposite of anarchy: its structure and premise tend to safeguard conservative values against the tremors of change. The criminal is discovered and expelled from the world in which he or she has been operating, leaving behind the frisson of remembered terror which only makes the protected environment more attractive.

For a genre centred on sin, death, grisly clues, fear, guilt and betrayals, the detective novel has been surprisingly cleansed of the real horrors of the world. Corpses are more like cardboard cut-out figures on a Cluedo board, detection is more often than not an amateur's hobby. The American crime novel has been more concerned than the British with squalid and seedy elements of crime and with the murky features of detection: Chandler and Chandler-imitations set their novels in the dangerous streets and grotty bed-sits of big cities.

Detective novels have been known as male genres but not because they have predominantly been written by men. Women have been prominent as authors of crime since the 1920s and 1930s: Agatha Christie, Helen MacInnes, Ngaio Marsh, Josephine Tey, Patricia Wentworth, and Dorothy Sayers. Women have read detective novels just as much as men, possibly more. But, looking at the older generation of detective-novel writers or even at the new Queens of Crime, it can seem that they have done little to transform the politics of the genre itself. Agatha Christie might choose a female sleuth, alongside the moustachioed Poirot, to solve a mystery. But Miss Marples, rescued from the loneliness and public contempt or pity of spinsterdom, is an eccentric and passionless figure who does not suffer, merely observes, the sexual, economic and social problems facing women of her generation. Most of her colleagues in crime choose male detectives: Sayers's whimsical Peter Whimsey, Marsh's handsome Alleyn, or Margery Allingham's deceptively bland

Campion. In detective novels as in no other genre, women writers can invent a male alter ego with impunity – a double-edged strategy of subversion and self-concealment. Further-more, these writers uphold as stalwartly as the male crime writers the ethos of their age: class, taste, an old-world social structure, a romantic nostalgia for a rural idyll of England long gone. Economic hierarchies, the fortresses of family, heterosexuality and monogamy, the whole moral dogmatic order operating in a simplified moral universe, are all the approved social codes that are threatened by the crime. In an age of uncertainty and anxiety, the morally simplistic structures of detective fiction can serve as palliatives.

Even in the 1980s, it cannot be taken for granted that the many distinguished women writers of detective fiction, most notably P.D. James, Patricia Highsmith and Ruth Rendell, infiltrate and subvert the genre with a female politics or a sexual perspective.

P. D. James writes detective novels of high literary quality and, especially with the psychologically pessimistic and distinctly un-cosy *A Taste for Death*, she has done much to revitalise the genre. Even if her books are founded on an essential conservatism – the realignment of traditional morals, the supremacy of the law, and the victory of innocence over evil – they have become progressively more concerned with the murky edges of crime. Around the comforting centre – the puzzle at the heart of the book which is solved – are a whole range of contemporary and social issues which cannot be solved and which often mean that the innocent are more hurt than the guilty. Abortion, reproduc-tive rights and the welfare state bureaucracy are as much the subjects of her writing as the uniquely disruptive murder.

Phyllis Dorothy White, alias P. D. James, was born in Oxford in 1920 and spent her childhood in Cambridge. Like her amateur sleuth Cordelia Grey, she was cut off from formal education when her father, a middle-grade civil servant 'not disposed to educating women', removed her from Cambridge High School at the age of sixteen. She married a doctor when she was twenty and gave birth to two daughters, but her husband returned from the war suffering from incurable schizophrenia. Faced with the task of supporting her family, P. D. James became a hospital administrator. She began to write a couple of years before her husband died. *Cover Her Face* was motivated not by financial but by emotional and psychological need. The tone set there of pervasive melancholy, and of the recognition that crime may have solutions but human suffering does not, has been strengthened over subsequent years. In *A Taste for Death* this is most evident and unrelieved. The crime, as well as many of the characters, is at times almost incidental, acting as a vehicle for human concerns: the horror of violent death, the poignant suffering of abandoned children, the emotional difficulty of being a single woman and the realities of class privilege and sexual prejudice. It is, as she says, an exploration of 'the bridges of law and order over a great chaos of both personal and psychological disorder', and it offers glimpses into insoluble human pains and unpunishable human betrayals.

P. D. James's novels, though they are written under a distancing and de-gendered pseudonym, are potent with a distinctly female acuity and eye for personal detail. They do not, however, take up a 'feminist' position. Nor do the novels of Patricia Highsmith which, although sold under the lucrative label of 'detective', are more psychological thrillers. They deal with the uglier and more repressed emotions that explode into crime; the puzzle at their heart is not 'who' but 'why' dunit. Her sequence of *Ripley* books, in which the completely amoral figure of Ripley is the psychopathic, foul and charming anti-hero, presents the reader with an unsettling and sinister vision of the moral universe: under the firm surface of right and wrong lurks and slithers the nastier, deeper world where moral absolutes collapse. Patricia Highsmith's novels and short stories do present us with portraits of obsessive misogyny and profound social sickness. But her own position remains unclear: she seems like a puppeteer, or a coldly curious scientist who 'likes to put individuals under strain' to see how they will react. Men are usually at the rotten centres of her nasty tales, but her female characters are often shown in negative, ambivalent or ironic lights.

She and Ruth Rendell both mark the movement of the detective novel away from their traditional function as palliatives to social anxiety. While still comforting readers with the promise of mystery and solution and the restoration of order, their moral vision is unsettling and complex.

The modern crime novels of Ruth Rendell, Patricia Highsmith and P. D. James no longer return us to an enclosed Garden of Eden, but allow the winds of change and terror to blow through its razed walls. Ruth Rendell is a politically progressive writer who has tackled the themes of feminism several times. Her early novels are set in a small village with a village copper investigating crimes motivated by incest, abuse, lesbianism and contemporary female ambitions. Lately she has written other books under the pseudonym of Barbara Vine. They centre on the mysteries of human motivation rather than the technical puzzles of detection. She has led her loyal readers from the closed world of detection to the more dangerous realms of psychological thriller written from a woman's perspective. Her female culprits are also victims of their age. Writing as Barbara Vine in *A Dark-Adapted Eye*, she tells the story of two sisters in the 1950s. Both are highly conventional and genteely repressed, and they are in possession of a shameful secret that invades the polished interiors of their respectable home. Behind lace curtains, over tea trays and delicate embroidery, they conduct a fierce and ritualised battle that must end in murder.

Ruth Rendell moves from the confining structures of traditional detection in order to write her more radical novels about the nature and motive of crime. Although a book like *A Dark-Adapted Eye* shares some of the characteristics of her previous novels – most importantly, a small and claustrophobic society destabilised by murder – it no longer uses the figure of its male sleuth to distance the narrative. The narrator of *A Dark-Adapted Eye* is an implicated female relative of the two embattled sisters; the story is not given to the reader by a dispassionate observer but filtered through emotion and faulty memory; the crime is not revealed, intact, but groped at through partial clues. The secret remains, ultimately, a secret. Such a tale cannot be contained by the detective form.

Other women writers of the 1980s have chosen to remain within the form – or have moved into it – but have given to the old conservative genre an explicitly radical and feminist content. Gone are the male detectives. In their wake come the consciously modern crusading female sleuths: Antonia Fraser's defiantly promiscuous and independent Jemima Shore; the attractively hedonistic Kate Fansler in the novels by Amanda Cross (pseudonym of the American feminist academic Carolyn Heilbrun); Mary Wings' lesbian heroine Emma Victor, unwillingly drawn into detection; Barbara Wilson's lesbian sleuth from Seattle, Pam Nilsen, battling alone against the forces of patriarchy; Gillian Slovo's very modern saxophonist-sleuth Kate Baeier; Liza Cody's buoyant creation Anna Lee . . . What is striking about all of these 1980s detectives, with the exception of the very modern but not so right-on Jemima Shore, is not just that they are explicitly feminist, and usually exploring male crimes against women, but that they are also involved, implicated, and personally agonised by the crimes that they solve. No longer do male detectives build up dossiers, draw up charts and discuss likely culprits over pints of beer in the local or cups of tea with 'the wife'. Instead, ideologically committed women risk their safety to find the solution because they see the crime as an example of patriarchy at large.

Moreover, in most traditional detective novels the detective is an agent of the law-abiding and fundamentally decent society. In these feminist versions, however, the detective is often a lonely and driven figure who pits herself against society: it is the existing moral order that is the real criminal behind each act of violence. So, in Barbara Wilson's novels, the feminist sleuth Pam Nilsen is a critic of American society. Her second mystery, *Sisters of the Road*, is set in the ugly underworld of Seattle into which Pam is unwillingly drawn. Offering a lift to two teenage prostitutes hitching outside a sleazy hotel, she finds herself with a corpse and a runaway on her hands and conscience. She feels implicated in the young fugitive's fate, and sets out in a desperate hunt to reach her young friend before the unknown killer. *Sisters of the Road* tackles issues of prostitution, poverty, child abuse and lesbian politics. Pam Nilsen's search is not simply a route through clues towards discovery (she is in fact a clumsy and bungling amateur sleuth) but a journey into her own psychology. While she unravels ugly crimes, she also delves into her own lesbian identity. Clues are metaphysical as well as actual; the amateur sleuth puts herself as well as patriarchal society on trial.

Sisters of the Road is a peculiarly and frustratingly hybrid novel: it bears the imprint of the angst-ridden and emotionally naked lesbian confessional, working its feminist concerns into the structure of a traditional detective story. Curiously, it also carries an atmosphere not dissimilar to the mean streets of Chandler's stories. Pam Nilsen is, like Philip Marlowe, solitary, world-weary and urbane, concealing a self ridden with doubt and interrogation. And, while she is a victim as well as a survivor in the sleazy underworld of violence and violation, her sexual forays and lonely voyages through the badlands of crime have a predatory tinge. Barbara Wilson's detective stories are contemporary feminist fables: rooted in introversion and uncertainty, driven by a morality which is continually questioned, they place both victim and detective in a solitary position. The community in *Sisters of the Road* is the community of the criminal.

But the ambivalence of Barbara Wilson's message is, still, embedded in the confident form of crime and detection. And whether the reader agrees with the ideology of her books or not, they will keep turning the pages until they reach the end's satisfaction. Barbara Wilson says that the structure as well as the explicit feminist position of her crime books are political choices, although she began almost by chance.

> What I was interested in was trying to find ways of
> talking about political ideas in a way that wasn't
> offputting. I was interested in how a genre could be used
> in a new way and expectations could be changed if it was
> a woman who was in that role.

She is adamant that feminist crime novels are politically important: they draw unaffiliated readers into feminism in a way that a work of innovative political theory cannot.

Barbara Wilson's Pam Nilsen is an explicitly alternative sleuth – lesbian, attached to communal living, eating health foods and wearing sensible clothes. And Barbara Wilson's detective novels are published in Britain by The Women's Press, emphasising again their self-conscious feminism. But a new style of female sleuth – modern, cool, witty, assertive and very much a product of the late 1980s – seems to be emerging, best represented by a writer from the United States, Sara Paretsky. Paretsky is a mainstream detective novelist; indeed, when *Killing Orders* was published it received a front-page interview in *The New York Times Book Review*, which is an extremely rare accolade for a mystery writer. In Britain she is published in hardback by Gollancz, and in paperback by Penguin, and read by a wide readership. Her female sleuth Vic Warshawski is a likeable and familiar figure: an engaging mixture of 1960s optimism and 1980s laid-back scepticism. Vic wears expensive Italian shoes and eye make-up; she likes men in her bed and good whisky in her drinks cabinet. And neither Vic nor her creator Paretsky are out to score ideological points – the reader does not feel, as with Barbara Wilson, that there is a lesson embedded in the scattered clues or a moralism wound into the tension. Instead, Paretsky's detective novels simply evolve out of a shrewd feminist consciousness. They are political novels in the sense that any novel written by a politically engaged novelist must be.

Vic Warshawski has some British contemporaries. Joan Smith's first detective novel, *A Masculine Ending*, is a literate, witty and well-written tale. Its sleuth is the feminist academic Loretta Lawson, who loathes structuralism, abhors deconstruction and makes an anxious and unwilling detective. Smith is self-conscious and self-deprecating: she takes a good many swipes at white, middle-class feminists (whom she represents), at academics (whom she also represents), and at detection. *A Masculine Ending* escapes the tinges of worthiness which mark a writer like Barbara Wilson by its wry, dry tone. Its explicit feminism is not agonised and self-searching but poised and sharply mocking.

In spite of the refreshing tales from Sara Partesky or Joan Smith, however, feminist detective novels often bear the hall-mark of so many series. Many mediocre or bad feminist crime novels are brought out on the tails of its popularity; many are stiff with ideological intention. The tendency for the trail of sym-bolically gendered clues to lead to an evil misogynist male is a stale feminist device. And when women take on the genre as a platform for their politics rather than writing as feminists from within it, they endanger its political possibilities. For the detec-tive novel is popular precisely because its familiarity comforts. In its movement away from the palliative of social anxieties to barometer of social ills it treads a precarious path, simultaneously fulfilling and upsetting the reader's expectations, and offering a risky mix of comfort and discomfort. The bleak moral climate and brutally realistic depictions of death of a P.D. James, the feminist conundrums and harsh realities of a Ruth Rendell, and the crusading and confessional spirit of a Barbara Wilson are powerful and liberating as long as they obey the rules. The reader's desire for the intellectual stimulation of pursuit, followed by the comfort and closure of detection, must be satisfied. Moral ambivalence is permissible if imaginatively rendered – moral didacticism is not.

Romance and the blockbuster

Nowhere is the debate between popularity and innovation more of a quicksand than with romance and raunchy blockbusters. It is summed up by the anxiety about the popularity of Mills & Boon books. How, ask feminist writers, can we be so contemptuous of books that are sold to millions of women readers all round the world? It is not good enough to say that consumers of stan-dardised romance are passive repositories, empty vessels into which debilitating ideas are poured. But, even though M & B place women's domestic experience at the centre of life, it is hard to absorb them into feminism, as some feminists have attempted. They offer, with a comforting and regressive simplicity, a dominant social vision: that, for women, intimate companionship means male sexual companionship, and that a woman's real power resides in her power to attract a man.

The M & B formula can appropriate some of the trappings of feminism, but it cannot really accommodate feminism. Could there be a M & B with a lesbian romance at its centre, or a plot which revolves around a sexually experienced older woman courting a younger man? No. And this 'no' eats its way into the more sexually explicit and elastic blockbusters, because they too feed fantasies that are far from radical or transforming. As soon as they are appropriated by feminism they become something else – no longer the kind of book that sells in its millions to the kind of reader usually resistant to sexual politics.

We all know what a romantic blockbuster implies. It is big, for a start – not the kind of book you can comfortably carry around with you; more the kind you keep beside the bed. It is glossily packaged, frequently with embossed glittering jackets, display-ing plunged cleavages and long legs ending in a stiletto heel. And then it has a fast-moving plot involving money, power, senti-mental 'true' love (always heterosexual), sex or a sex-substitute (usually money). There is a hero (rich, grim, powerful and with concealed wells of tenderness beneath his manly chest); a heroine (beautiful, often poor-becoming-rich, often an orphan or without family support); a huge amount of consumerism – clothes, objects and possessions are described in intricate detail; a fair sprinkling of misunderstanding and jealousy and melodrama.

The blockbusters of the 1970s and 1980s are a far cry from the Cartland-esque tales of quivering and sickly innocence, where untouched and virginal little-girl heroines attract the necrophiliac lusts of big rich heroes. In many ways blockbusters are far less sexually offensive than Cartland's novels, with their frank sexual desires, powerful and experienced female protagonists and rejec-tion of the romantic self-sacrifice and mute obedience which make Cartland's novels into suppurating tales of extreme female oppression. But if Barbara Cartland-type Gothic romance is a modern rendering of bowdlerised fairy tales, feeding twentieth-century fantasies (of 'back to the home', 'back to the virtues of virginity and female dependency'), the new romances can also be read as twentieth-century fairy tales. Their 'happily ever after' is often, admittedly, endlessly deferred (family sagas are a popular subsection of the genre, and cannot therefore have a simple ending in marriage). But its presence is implied. And the 'happy ever after' is not reached simply through the traditional revelation of undying love and the promise of marriage. What these modern heroines unashamedly aspire to is wealth and power – they are empire builders (business empires, and family empires through whom the blood and story line can be continued). They are rags-to-riches heroines for the 1980s.

Barbara Taylor Bradford's blockbusters have enjoyed phenomenal sucess – *A Woman of Substance*, her first novel, has sold well over 20 million copies worldwide. The 'woman of substance', Emma Harte, represents twentieth-century aspirations and values, for she is superwoman. She begins as humble servant girl, deceived by the master, and ends up as tycoon, all through her own indomitable will. Beautiful and loving and shrewd, she is the austere business woman by day and good in bed at night. Barbara Taylor Bradford appeals to the American Dream of individual attainment, softened by the romance of the English past and its rigid class system. It is power, reached through individual effort ('You too,' the book says, 'could be like this'), that makes Emma Harte sexy. For, although there is a great deal of love interest in Barbara Taylor Bradford's novels, their carefully detailed opulence is far more seductive than any caress; climaxes are reached in boardrooms rather than in bedrooms. Barbara Taylor Bradford's heroines want everything – and they get it.

Sally Beauman's *Destiny* bears more resemblance to a Jackie Collins than to a Barbara Taylor Bradford novel. Set in Britain, America, and numerous glamorous European travel spots; spinning a familiar tale of sex, greed, power and betrayal; portraying an aristocratic and cold hero (yes, with a big heart concealed beneath an unsmiling face) and a stunning heroine, *Destiny* holds in its 800 pages all the ingredients of a bestseller. But it also displays just how disquieting a bodice-ripper, aimed at women readers and avowedly 'feminist' in its portrayal of powerful women, can be. The goal is untold wealth and undying love – hero and heroine trample over hoards of secondary characters in order to get there. Sex is a grisly, priapic and brutal business, in which someone always seems to be exploited. The heroine starts life as an innocent and passive victim (at one point she allows her obsessed suitor to make love to her while she is apparently asleep – the nearest you can get to the necrophiliac romance of Sleeping Beauty), and travels towards a more active and exploitative role.

Looking at blockbusters by writers such as Sally Beauman or Barbara Taylor Bradford, and taking into account the readers' expectations, it is hard to see how they can be injected with feminism in the same way as detective novels have been. The conventions of the bodice-rippers are all tied to the attractions of power, the possibility of the perfect heterosexual union, and to a world of rampant consumerism. If blockbusters have broken away from stereotypical sexual relations, in which the man is dominant and the woman sweetly dependent, they nevertheless present another set of 1980s stereotypes – that woman can (and should) be superwoman and that the exercise of huge power is all right so long as women can do it too.

But romantic blockbusters, historical and family sagas, are read in their thousands by millions of women. It is not surprising that, lured by their mass appeal, feminists have taken up the genre. Jill Tweedie has written a fat romantic novel, *Bliss*, which highlights the difficulties of infiltrating and subverting a genre so steeped in anti-feminist assumptions. From an automatic assumption, held in ignorance, that 'that kind of book' was not her kind of book, she started to reappraise her dismissive attitude, asking herself,

> Why had I so confidently rubbished books I had never
> read? Was that not tantamount to rubbishing the millions
> of readers of those books? And if I did that, how could I
> consider myself remotely 'left-wing', remotely in the
> business of championing the causes of the many against
> the elite few?

So she started to read: first Jackie Collins ('the best of her genre') and then the first chapter of other bodice-rippers, with 'their cardboard characters, their lumpen dialogue and their obsession with brand names'. And she thought,

> Almost all blockbusters are about the mega-rich and famous . . . but suppose as many readers could be informed, via the blockbuster, about the lives of the poor and disinherited or about the great issues of our time, the issues that threaten the survival of all of us, whether we are aware of them or not?

Jill Tweedie set herself to tackle the question in practice: does a bestseller have to be escapist, or can it be concerned with something a little more vital than the comings and goings of the beautiful, the rich and the rightly damned?

Bliss contains many of the familiar escapist ingredients: beautiful young heroine, mysterious and sinister older man, sex, money, power and an exotic background. 'And when,' Jill Tweedie says, 'I thought I had caught my reader, I broke some of the rules. The beautiful heroine becomes involved with the poor Indian women in her husband's fiefdom, she discovers his dastardly plot against them, she acts to foil it.' Halfway through the book, the formula radically changes direction: into politics and power games, and the machinations of the CIA. The beautiful heroine becomes political and not interested in romantic love, self-fulfilment or personal trauma; the sinister older man is revealed to be sinister through and through without that concealed tenderness. The blockbuster is turned inside out as thoroughly as a glove – for the ends to which it aspires oppose those of its predecessors. Where money, power, and heterosexual and individual fulfilment have been the accepted goals of a traditional blockbuster, here the goals are a disruption of power on behalf of the powerless, a rejection of wealth as a form of satisfaction and a turning away from the 'bliss' of heterosexuality towards a sisterly solidarity with the heroine's less fortunate sisters.

But *Bliss*, while it did sell many thousands of copies, never really attained the bestsellerdom of the 'real' romantic block-buster. And those readers who did buy *Bliss* were probably *Guardian*-reading Tweedie-followers, rather than the block-buster-consuming mass that Jill Tweedie had in mind. She was mainly preaching to the converted. Moreover, her novel wore its ideological intentions so visibly that few readers could have failed to recognise the novel as a sugared pill, ostensibly written to entertain, actually to instruct. Jill Tweedie did not write a potboiler because that was the kind of book she liked and knew she could write; she wrote it for strategic feminist reasons which infect the novel with a kind of finger-wagging didacticism.

Her attitude poses a seemingly irresolvable problem. Women writers who see the world from a feminist perspective do not usually want to write a blockbuster; they do not like the form or the rules but are only tempted by the opportunities provided by a huge readership. How can they then expect a huge readership? Novels like *Bliss*, which seek to convert by entertaining, are searching up a cul-de-sac of feminism for that elusive vehicle, a radical novel that holds mass appeal.

Popular form and radical intent

The family sagas of Zoë Fairbairns are straightforward, enter-taining and shrewd examples of feminism reworking a popular form without being flattened by the dead hand of ideological opportunism. The form that she has chosen is particularly suited to her recurring moral preoccupations. Her novels (including *Benefits, Stand We At Last* and *Closing*) try to blend the popular and the complex. Within them, her female characters grapple with the difficulties and inevitable compromises of being female in a man's world and of juggling pragmatism with emotional and political integrity. A novel like *Closing* is full of ambivalence and spiked with questions which cannot find a single answer. One of the most dominant and insistent queries is, 'Is selling selling out?', or, 'Are you feminist or are you commercial?' Zoë Fairbairns manages to straddle the gulf between the two because she has always wanted to write about the relationships between men and women and she genuinely likes the family saga form. When she sits down in her study (a room of her own, whose address only two other people know) she is preoccupied by the details of plot and difficulties of dialogue, rather than the political effect of her message. When she talks about her own work, she insists that her novels, like her feminism, evolve from her moral and emotional preoccupations, rather than being dictated by them.

Zoë Fairbairns successfully injects a popular form with a radical message, and she has won an appreciative readership. Because she did not take up the genre as an ideological campaign, the fact that she does not sell in huge numbers does not invalidate her work. She is nowhere near the airport-blockbuster league. She is a far better craftswoman than most writers of best-selling blockbusters – her plots are more compulsive and credible, her preoccupations more intriguing and her characters fuller – but her sales will never rival theirs. Zoë Fairbairns apparently proves that it is the ingredients of a blockbuster that matter, even more than their formulaic structure. Her novels lack the necessary descriptions of graphic sex, epic greed and moral simplicity. A writer has to obey the detailed rules as well as the general format of the traditional blockbuster or saga in order to reach the large and loyal audience enjoyed by Collins, Krantz *et al*.

The fear that it is impossible to be genuinely radical and illuminating within a traditional and popular form is countered by the examples of the North American writers Marilyn French and Marge Piercy. They have been models and forerunners, writers who invested the blockbuster with radicalism and who managed to grip their many readers in a racy tale while illuminating and even transforming their readers' lives. Both French and Piercy, coming from a background of the civil rights movement and first-wave feminism, have written books for the women they once were. Their novels are familiar 'good reads' and yet are angry, impassioned and morally crusading, catching and feeding the mood of the time, articulating women's dissatisfaction with their lot and earning the blurb on their jackets: 'This book will change women's lives'.

The Women's Room was published in 1977. It is the story of Mira Ward, a wife of the 1950s who became a woman of the 1970s. Mira escapes from her life of diapers, suburban cocktail parties and dutiful weekly sex into a journey of feminist education. She discovers through her hard-won independence and her female friendships the exhilaration of liberation. *The Women's Room* is a fat, satisfying and fast-moving novel that aims for the solar plexus. Women are presented as victimised and courageous, men as infantile and, usually, brutal – little boys playing ugly power games. Through Mira and her friends Marilyn French explores the whole gamut of female oppressions. There is something in her novel for every woman: the drabness of suburban wifedom, the loneliness of independence, the horror of rape, the infantile regression of men, the possibility of escape and transformation.

And it is certainly true that *The Women's Room* generated enough emotional heat to 'change lives'. Marilyn French considers that its impact came because it was one of the first books that

> spelt the truth about how a lot of women felt. It wasn't a
> truth coming to them from the outside; it was a truth
> they had known, and felt, and never seen reflected in their
> culture. When they did see it they recognised it
> immediately and suddenly realised that they were not
> peculiar. The reason they were unhappy was not because
> they were neurotic or bad, but because these were cultural
> facts about what happens to women. It empowered them.
> The possession of truth is always empowering.

The tone of these sentences echoes the tone of the book. There is a missionary zeal to *The Women's Room*, a kind of nannyish hectoring. Marilyn French is giving us 'the truth' in all its monolithic and overpowering (rather than 'empowering') simplicity. Women readers – and a few male ones – responded to it as if their eyes had suddenly been opened to the blaze of the obvious. Some wrote to Marilyn French saying that now they realised they must find a job, leave their husbands, achieve sexual satisfaction, throw off their dependence. Men accused her of wrecking their marriages. The 'truth' of *The Women's Room* was its recognition that something was very wrong with the majority of women's lives; its success lay in its potboiler form.

Comforting us with the possibility of change and bludgeoning us with the power of its contemporary truths, the novel is written in the 1970s, for the 1970s – and remains a product of the 1970s, static in its certainties. Marilyn French's subsequent works have never achieved the power or success of her first novel. Her second novel, *The Bleeding Heart*, is nearly as trite as its title. Her theoretical work, *Beyond Power*, is a moral potboiler: a massive, urgent and deadening book that attempts to cast the fine mesh of feminist vision over the history of the world in an awesome and failed effort at synthesis. French starts out with an unfamiliar rural Eden, where fruit hangs from the trees, the grass is always green and there is no past. 'In the beginning was the Mother' and intimate matrocentric communities lived at one with Nature. Then comes the more familiar and fearsome world of patriarchy, a system built on the Word ('and the Word was a lie') and attempting to achieve supremacy over Nature through greed and tyrannical power. Natural and 'feminised' wisdom is pushed to the margins; structures of dominance, which all political systems espouse, force both men and women to lie against nature; to live in terror; compulsively to seek power and to torture and kill in order to get it. *Beyond Power* is very, very long and deafens with the click of its card index (Chapter 3 has 620 footnotes and the bibliography extends over forty-one pages). French bullies anthropology, science, medicine, philosophy, psychology, literature and myth into the shape of her argument, until the book becomes a nightmare version of Trivial Pursuits. But the hailstorm of facts never obliterates French's inimitable voice: she tells us, bosses us, warns us, insists on our 'moral revolution' in which we would 'seize our own areas of freedom'. She flattens feminism into a

138

matter of simple biological determinism and never seems in doubt of her own vision of the world.

Then came the long and lugubrious novel *Her Mother's Daughter*, in which the same voice hectors us. The moral certainty that energises her writing also places her readers in the nursery, where to disagree is to disobey. Once again, she invests a popular form with a moral content, choosing the family saga as a vehicle for her flat-footed and mournful vision: a world in which women lead tragic lives. *Her Mother's Daughter* tells of four generations of women, each of whom sacrifices her own life for her children's future. Shackled together by the umbilical cord, the four women perform a gloomy follow-my-leader down the century. Monumental, brooding, repetitious, nagging and obsessed, the novel is an inert mass of despair and, eventually, boredom. Nowhere does it display the ability of French's first novel to speak for millions of other women, or to capture the mood of the time.

But perhaps the mood of the 1980s is a difficult one to capture; its fragmented aspect is peculiarly unsuited to French's certainties. And unsuited too, it would seem to the fired politics of Marge Piercy. Piercy has always written books that are for and of their time, seeking to reflect the main issues and preoccupations of the generations through which she has lived. *Braided Lives* dealt with the 1950s, *Vida* and *Small Changes* with the 1960s, the intermingling of dystopia and utopia in *Woman on the Edge of Time* with the 1970s, *Fly Away Home* with the early 1980s. Of all of these, the latter is the least successful, because the least lit by rage and crusading zeal. Then in 1987 came a change of direction: Marge Piercy wrote a very long novel about the past.

Gone to Soldiers is an unwieldy tale of sacrifice and suffering in the Second World War. An enormous number of books published during the late 1980s have focused on the Second World War – is it just because forty-odd years is the right kind of time span to look back on the last total war? Is it nostalgia, in the secular confusion of the 1980s, for a time of (apparently) moral imperatives? Or the recognition, as we approach the millennium, of how the Second World War tore across this historically accelerated century – breaking up families, eroding class systems, challenging sexual mores, and at the same time initiating the post-Holocaust, post-Hiroshima age? In Britain the Beveridge Plan which opened the door to the welfare state, the Butler Education Act which opened the way to a new meritocracy, and the landslide victory of the Labour Government in 1945, all deeply changed the structure of society. An old way of life, and the old class which had administered it, seemed to be dying. And this mixture of absolutes and ambiguities, of glorification of human courage and anxiety about the human future, may be one reason why books about the war have been so abundant recently. The war years have always been invested with tragedy and heroism, attracting some fine and much appalling writing. It is a painful paradox that the war tragically enabled advances for women, the welfare state, increased mobility, and the prospect of full employment. That those things are under attack is a rich subject for writers. Certainly it is a subject to which, in the last few years, women writers have increasingly turned (Maureen Duffy's *Changes* and Valerie Miner's *In the Company of Women* are two of the many novels in 1987 to join the mass of books by men about the Second World War). They have taken up war, traditionally a subject for male writers, and invested it with their own particular vision.

Marge Piercy believes that the novel is her finest achievement, but *Gone to Soldiers* wastes the fictional opportunities and contemporary urgencies found in the Second World War. Telling of the war from an American perspective, but bogged down by its great length and apparently exhaustive research, it is neither intelligent nor original. A huge cast of characters is flung across the globe, so that most of the worst events of the war can be described: one character is in the Resistance, another witnesses the aftermath of Hiroshima, another goes to the concentration camps. But the war is simply an exaggerated backdrop to human emotions; Piercy fails to deal with the huge changes that war brought to our world. The break-up of society is dealt with in banal ways: rules of sexual behaviour, for instance, are eroded simply in response to the heart-tugging plea, 'Tomorrow I may be dead.' It is clear that Marge Piercy intends a denunciation of the war and all its macho values. But she succumbs to enticing absolutes: there is heroism or cowardice, innocence or culpability. Under the apparent modernism of the book's fragmented structure is the roar of good and evil. And this is astonishing, for the power of Piercy's writing has come from the purity and complexity of her rage. In *Gone to Soldiers* she is no longer investing an established form with the stark voice of opposition; the absence of this compelling disjuncture makes the fat and nostalgic novel into a thin and disappointing fiction.

The traditional saga and the romance, however soaked in contemporary mores and however immersed in the consumer greed of the 1980s, possess a certainty of form and aspiration. They are modern fairy tales for an age of confusion. Feminist blockbusters, aiming to subvert the genre, pit themselves against the reassurances of continuing traditional values, and the probability of an individual 'happy-ever-after'. One of the qualities that feminism does *not* possess at the moment is certainty; nor has it ever attempted to act as a palliative for an uncertain age. Marilyn French wrote *The Women's Room* during a decade that, in spite of its manifold oppressions, held out hope of profound change. *Her Mother's Daughter*, a defeated and world-weary book, is a novel for the late 1980s. Marge Piercy wrote novels in the 1960s and 1970s that are fired by their present; her novels of the 1980s are soaked in a strange nostalgia, a kind of privileged decay. Perhaps her tenacious statement that neither her feminism nor her radicalism has changed over the decades points to the problem. Or maybe writers no longer want to produce, nor readers to consume, the moral potboilers that two decades ago could illuminate and transform lives.

Science fiction

Science fiction used to be dominated by tales of bug-eyed monsters and aliens from other planets. They reflected a male enthusiasm for the technologies of domination. Employing the simple equation between technological advance and 'progress',

141

they were often fables of conquering new worlds and seemed to replace the imperial romance. Now planets, rather than other countries, could be overcome, controlled and laid to waste. Such fantasies are peopled by very few women.

Unlike detective novels or romance, science fiction is not a fixed genre. Its rules are those not of form, but of imagination. The science fiction writer must project her novel into a future, performing an act of prophecy and commenting upon the way we live now. It is a genre that seems ideal for feminist invasion: a ready-made laboratory in which feminists may explore possibilities, issue warnings and play with ideas about how society could be restructured. Both male and female writers of science fiction have largely deserted the cartoon stories of spaceships, lunar landscapes and things that go bump in the night and turned instead to the more socially engaged end of the genre: the future as a short step and sharp comment upon now; the future as a world in which we already live.

With its potential for unleashing the political imagination and for hypothesising about the near future, science fiction has been a boom area for feminist writers over the last two decades. It is more naturally a political genre than crime or romantic fiction, and many of the feminist science fictions that have recently been published contain a hard-line feminist politics. It is also a genre that will more easily absorb ideological theories into its structure. Many female practitioners have used the form as an analysis of feminism, a critique of patriarchy and an examination of ways forward into a better future for women and humankind.

Herein lies its strength and weakness. The opportunity the genre provides for thoughtful writers to work through their preoccupations in fictional form is also the trap it springs upon more dogmatic writers, who become locked into empty rhetoric, banal theory and feminist cliché. Science fiction is an arena for what Maureen Duffy calls the 'hypothesising imagination'; hence the quality of feminist science fiction is a useful if crude barometer for the current climate of feminist thought.

It points to patchy weather. The most compelling science fiction, written by writers such as Lisa Tuttle, Ursula Le Guin,

Joanna Russ, Gwyneth Jones, and experimented with by many others (Maureen Duffy, Doris Lessing, Marge Piercy, Zoë Fairbairns, Margaret Atwood), presents a future in which the struggle is continuous and interesting. It has at its source an intelligent and urgent feminist projection of the present.

One of the best known and most respected of feminist science fiction writers is the North American Joanna Russ, who combines radical feminism with literary post-modernism. Her most interesting novel, *The Female Man*, is a subversive analysis of the power that men have over women. Like Marge Piercy's *Woman on the Edge of Time*, it co-mingles present and future. But where Marge Piercy has one central protagonist, Connie, who in the present is a drugged and helpless inmate of a mental hospital and yet can enter a utopian future of ecological and hermaphroditic harmony, Joanna Russ fragments her central character. Acknowledging our fractured identity, she splits herself into four different narrators (all of whose names begin with 'J') to play out four simultaneous worlds. There is the self-named Joanna of the present, struggling in a man's world; Jeannine the romantic dreamer from an altered past where the Second World War never happened and the Great Depression continues; Janet from the planet Whileaway, where no men have lived for over a hundred years; and finally Jael who hopes to unite all the Js. Russ's novel is conversational, witty and fragmented. Its enraged polemicism is offset by a delightful vulgarity and rueful self-mockery. Such rude rupturing of literary conventions makes *The Female Man* into a science fiction which is pervaded by idiosyncratic feminism at all levels. The structural fragmentation makes it into an intellectual pursuit in which options and alternatives overlap, rather than a straightforward prophecy.

With its multiple plots, preoccupations and cerebral fascinations, *The Female Man* also demonstrates the great appeal that science fiction holds for women writers and their readers. They are adventure stories with women as their heroines. They are tales that stand outside society as we know it and therefore outside received and patriarchal versions of our present and future. They can explore links between biology and culture, between the constructed and innate. They can be boldly moral and speculative fables for our times.

Contrasting with the sophisticated and shrewd speculations of writers like Joanna Russ or Ursula Le Guin are the proliferating feminist science fictions that reduce the genre to its lowest common denominator and freeze feminist debate into a parody of itself. Over the last decade the women's presses have published many terrible novels which take place in a future apparently disconnected from the present. Many of those feminist science fictions are ghastly utopias, tedious in their unchanging female perfection and sentimental in their belief in a matriarchal world without violence, conflict, competition, litter, or a single cross word or dark shadow. They are the novels of 'herstories' and 'nightstallions': sloppy, pious feminist fables, tyrannised by biological determinism. The simple belief that the problems of the world are all caused by men and would swiftly be solved if there were no men around exemplifies a knee-jerk feminism at its most complacent and unattractive. The acute yearning which clogs up many of the narratives – for a tender, caring, motherly society – reflects women's dissatisfaction with the brutal realities of contemporary life. But the alternative is presented as so unerotic and tedious that it diminishes rather than illuminates current anxieties.

Such feminist novels neither explore possible futures nor criticise the present. Rather, they are fictional versions of wishful thinking, heavy with nostalgia for a world which is not, never was and never will be. They might be interesting to devotees of science fiction, and curious as a pointer to the way some women are dealing with their current disaffections. But as works of literature or as contributions to feminist theory, they advance nothing.

Just as, at one end of its genre, detective novels tend to flow into the psychological thriller, so science fiction has a fascinating overlap. Futurism is a realm in which the imagination can work according to the writer's own rule. Unlike much science fiction, a futurist novel does not take place in an artificially constructed world, but in a world constructed out of the present.

It is a breath away from today, and we have the sense, when reading it, that we are already living in our future.

The novels populating the area of overlap between science fiction and futurism are difficult to cordon off. However, a number of women writers who had previously written realist fiction have recently turned to the science fiction and futurist genres, and exploited their premises and conventions. One of the most obvious and arresting results is the rise of the dystopia as a distinct literary category.

The 1960s and 1970s were decades for utopias. With the flowering of feminism there was a sense that anything was possible – that we could achieve brave new worlds. In the 1980s, the sense of fragile but powerful possibility has largely been replaced by uncertainty, gloom and fear for the future. There was, fleetingly, a literature by women that said, 'This is what we can achieve,' which is now being replaced by a literature that more often than not says, 'This is what can happen to us if we continue along this path.' Even the word 'dystopia' hardly existed fifteen years ago; now it is commonly used to describe the imaginative rendering of our nightmares. Challenge has given way to warning.

The bleakness of warning is potent in Margaret Atwood's dystopia *The Handmaid's Tale*. She takes the proposition, 'a woman's place is in the home', and follows it to its logical ends. In the novel's imagined society, a patriarchal coup is effected economically; women's credit cards are no longer valid and they have no access to money in their own right. So Atwood's land of Gilead is born, founded on misogyny and the state control of desire, where women are handmaids, Marthas, whores or wives. Marriages are arranged, there is no divorce, and homosexuality is outlawed.

Although the novel describes a world of male/female functionality, the handmaid Offred's narration is not diagrammatic. It reveals a complex range of women's responses to their predicament, from acquiescence and collaboration to extreme and decisive rejection. Margaret Atwood uses her Orwellian prison narrative as a comment upon current social dangers and the fractured state of female politics. *The Handmaid's Tale* focuses upon the vulnerabilities of the present, acting as a warning to anybody who believes that advances made by women cannot be turned back.

It is not entirely bleak. The narrator herself, on the run from the authorities, offers her dissenting voice and belief that individuals can be effective. Speaking out of an enforced silence, she states her faith that there is an alternative world to Gilead: 'I keep on going with this hungry and sad and sordid, this limping and mutilated tale, because after all I want you to hear it . . . I'm at last believing in you. I'm believing you into being.' Such a statement is a gesture of trust towards the unknown reader: that we will respond, and imagine what it is like to be somewhere else that is simultaneously here and now. Anxious and complex, the novel uses some of the features of science fiction to express passionate commitment to, and rejection of, a science-fiction present.

It seems almost inevitable that the possibilities for speculation offered by science fiction should appeal to writers who feel themselves to be the truth-tellers or Cassandras of an unenlightened age. Doris Lessing is almost the role model of such a writer. Initially hailed as a spokeswoman for women and subsequently criticised for her attacks upon the left (most notably in *The Good Terrorist*), she has consistently surprised readers by her fierce self-questioning and her use of diverse genres. She has rarely been a strictly realist writer. *The Golden Notebook* is full of realist blandishments – the novel opens and closes with the now-familiar scene of two women in a kitchen talking about their particularly female concerns – but it actually takes off from realism. It is a literary experiment that questions the nature of the novel – an exploration of feminism, politics and madness. In it the central character, Anna, plays a game of cosmic dilation that eventually unhinges her. Sitting in her room, she takes its apparently insignificant contents, then progressively withdraws from them, moving further and further into 'space' and regarding the diminished earth from a great disengagement.

The Four-Gated City, the final novel in the *Children of Violence* series, takes this investigation of inner and outer spaces one stage further. Beginning in the rancid and realistic interior of a London fish and chip shop, it ends by observing London from an extreme futurist distance – a series of extra-territorial communities in which the survivors of apocalypse build their brave new world. In *Memoirs of a Survivor* Lessing places her story of terrifying urban disintegration in a near-future, depicting the gradual domination of the city by mobs of streetwise teenagers and children. It is a futurist novel that is about contemporary inner-city blight and hostility between youth and adulthood. Her preoccupation with psychic forces and with the impact of world events upon helpless individuals should have prepared her readers for her galactic chronicle *Canopus in Argos Archives*.

The *Canopus* chronicle leaves behind petty individual and nationalist squabbles and sets itself up as an epic of sociology and anthropology. Its characters are reminiscent of figures from the old Nordic sagas or the Old Testament and the purpose of the archives is to record the future. It is a difficult, mathematical and disengaged work, a far cry from the appealing earlier novels in which minute particulars hook on to larger themes. And, in fact, Lessing is hardly a novelist any more in these science fiction adventures – rather she is a chronicler and soothsayer, examining the entrails of contemporary society for the shape of things to come.

The increased use of genre-writing by women writers is a welcome development, heralding a newly accommodating stage in which feminism can be flippant as well as serious, in which women can admit to enjoying romantic blockbusters, or to being hooked on crime. But, in themselves, detective novels, science fictions, romances and sagas are not intellectual or literary developments. They are not usually on literature's or feminism's front line of change. They are the products and stimulants of clever packaging as well as the consequence of relieved acceptance by feminists of attitudes and pleasures previously policed by a sterner feminist ideology.

The feminist novels that most rigidly adhere to the conventions of their genre face grave difficulties. The structure of detection can be injected with feminism but not entirely subverted. The strict format of the romantic blockbuster hardly permits the kind of disruption that would transform its sexually oppressive message. Science fiction, if not powerfully and imaginatively rendered, quickly dates as a piece of ideological hectoring. It is when they are ruptured that genres become fascinating and challenging. There we can see some of the most interesting developments in women's writing taking shape. The psychological thriller that has been largely born out of the detective novel, or the futurist text that has been influenced by the conventions of science fiction, demonstrates that experiments are being made and risks taken. The plundering of genres by women writers is a vital activity in the creation of their own fictional realm. And more and more women writers are crossing genres, coupling them and collapsing them into each other. It is a step towards a newly ambitious and exciting women's literature – but, as yet, only a step.

seven

NEW FEMALE FORMS

────────

Realism's diaspora

Each slim and pleasing Anita Brookner novel is very much like the next. She has found her literary niche and seems intent on remaining there. And many feminist confessionals are also similarly predictable in their form and their concerns. This is not true of many of Brookner's British contemporaries. In the last few years particularly, established women who began writing in the pre-feminist 1960s and the early 1970s and who have been known, vaguely, as 'realist', have moved away from their familiar structures and started to experiment with new forms and ideas. It is a strange phenomenon. An older and more established generation of writers seems to have entered a new and bold phase of writing, rather than the daughters of feminism. Margaret Drabble, Elaine Feinstein, Doris Lessing, Nadine Gordimer, Antonia Byatt and Emma Tennant all started with realist novels that dealt with the plight of the individual within her society and have all, in the last few years, turned towards larger canvasses and themes. It is as if the constraints of contemporary domestic realism cannot bear the weight and breadth of their late-1980s preoccupations.

The need that some women writers now feel to review the past few decades and ask how we arrived at the society in which we live, rather than simply to evoke that society, is exemplified by Margaret Drabble's latest literary experiment, Margaret Drabble's novels have been published steadily since the early 1960s and have explored what it is like to be a woman living in modern times – though usually a white, Hampstead Heath-type woman. Her novels are the obvious and often-cited examples of British middle-class parochialism in literature. They are precise about time and place, firmly grounded in social reality and permeated by particular social issues: abortion, adultery, unwilling independence and resentful dependence, the approach of middle age, the betrayals of the 1960s and the disappointments of the 1970s.

The Radiant Way, written after the years of fictional silence when she was compiling *The Oxford Companion to English Literature*, is less rooted in a precise moment and altogether more ambitious in scope. It is Drabble's wry portrait of a generation (her generation) which has lived through the optimistic and profligate 1960s, the disappointed 1970s and the austere and lethargic 1980s. With a whole archive of newspaper cuttings and radio and TV broadcasts, and a great cast of characters – one-time radicals who are now arts administrators, one-time campaigning journalists who are now portly and complacent producers, one-time militant feminists who are now harassed mothers trying to maintain their marriages and careers – *The Radiant Way* is endlessly registering the impact of public life upon the politically aware. Hesitant, tolerant and socially concerned (the SDP – or SLD – of British literary experiments?), it is nevertheless bold in its summation of the spirit of the age. And the title is swiftly understood to be ironic: the radiant way is a road strewn with misery, disillusion, compromise or failure. The dreams of the 1960s are the advertising slogans of the 1980s; the fragmented and purposeless eclecticism of the 1970s has been briskly shaped into 'the new sense of realism'.

The Radiant Way is continually fascinating as a social documentary, and frequently wooden in its characterisation. But, in spite of its anxious and humanitarian mildness, it is an audacious attempt at cultural assessment – a state-of-the-nation novel, attempting to catch and frame our contemporary history as it hurtles past us, trying to give the reader a feel of what it is like to be alive today, in the Thatcherite 1980s. Behind us lie the decades of swift change and reversals, and a whole generation of 'the chosen, the elite, the garlanded of the great social dream' look back at themselves as idealistic youths as if at strangers. In front lies the absolute bewilderment of the future, promising and revealing little about itself, forcing that same generation to ask 'where do we go from here?'

Margaret Drabble's progress from the strictly realist prose of the 1970s to the adventurous and elastic form of *The Radiant Way* represents a growing dissatisfaction among many women writers of her generation with the constraints of realism – and, at the same time, a growing sense that the times require cultural spokeswomen: truth-tellers and soothsayers. For there is a way in which these older generation of women writers have taken upon themselves the role of cultural scientists and historians of the age. Doris Lessing has gradually deserted the solid and reassuring firmness of realism, which depends upon the reader's familiarity with what is being portrayed, for weirder and more symbolic territories: the descent into apocalypse with *The Four-Gated City*, the surreal nightmare of *Memoirs of a Survivor*, the dissection of the present in her complicated and depersonalised science fictions, the continuing exploration of 'normality' and alienation in her horror story *The Fifth Child*. Her most recent novels, with the exception of the pseudonymously published Jane Somers works, construct a thesis of social behaviour into which her characters then slot. Lessing's novels reject the idea of a 'natural' or 'normal' society, and question the existence of 'true' emotions, innate 'goodness' or 'absolute morality' – upon which the realist novel tends to rely.

The tendency to place characters with whom we can identify, and experiences with which we sympathise, in an unfamiliar social context is increasingly characteristic of several established writers. Maureen Duffy's first novel, *That's How It Was*, is 'almost exclusively – or inclusively – autobiographical'. An evocation of her childhood and a poignant tribute to the life and early death of her mother, it 'took up the burden of twenty-eight years' and was written as a consolation and 'a form of continuing life'. Her subsequent works do not possess the intimate and emotional subjectivity of *That's How It Was*, nor do they employ its realist methods. She has turned instead to other genres – science fiction, history, the spy novel, even an Ealing comedy – and other techniques, particularly the idiosyncratic mosaic style in which narratives are layered over each other.

Fay Weldon, who has always written tart satires on human behaviour, has become increasingly wayward and morally vituperative. The *Deus ex machina* is now an unashamed prop, the unlikely and apparently slapdash plot increasingly outrageous and inappropriate. Her characters have become less important so that her ideas – on the position of women, the horror of many men, and the nature of Britain's de-classed society – emerge more noisily. She almost parodies herself in an attempt to make herself heard above the din of her own clipped sentences. Emma Tennant, whose first novel was described by Alberto Moravia as an example of 'bourgeois decadence', now writes works of dystopia, satire and futurism. Iris Murdoch, who has always entangled her characters in a constructed world of moral dilemmas and spiritual absolutes, now makes little attempt to disguise the artificiality of plot. For such writers, realism can no longer contain the imagination.

Towards the millennium

The late 1980s have an unreal atmosphere, as if they have been ripped from their context. History is replaced by habit and nostalgia. The future is unknowable in a new sense, for we no longer have faith in it. And our alienation from the future is exaggerated by the approach of the year 2000, which has a ring of science fiction about it.

The words we use to describe the late 1980s demonstrate our cultural bafflement – they define the era both by what has gone before, and by what no longer exists: post-modernism, with its fragments, its parodies, its nightmare scenarios, its articulation of uncentred and soulless existences, its schizoid nature and lack of identity; post-historicism, which refers us back to events that tore across the century, leaving us to be jolted in its wake; post-feminism, post-Christian, post-traditional, post-AIDS, post-Holocaust, post-Hiroshima . . .

We are living in what comes after – the after-life which is a half-life. It is a strange thought that the history which defines our age has not been experienced by several generations. Most of us now did not live through, or have no memory of, war and depression, the horror of the concentration camps and the first nuclear bomb. But we are also living in what comes after – we are the pre-millennium, pre-nuclear, 'waiting for' generation.

Even things which are now happening, and which a generation or two ago we would have dismissed as the fantasies of political paranoia or futuristic fever, we now tend to take for granted. AIDS, Star Wars, *in vitro* fertilisation and surrogate motherhood, the planned privatisation of water and coal, proposed electronic identification cards and electronic tagging of criminals, intelligent robots, acid rain, the destruction of the ozone layer and of tropical rainforests, impenetrable information banks, computer hacking: such things, which gesture towards a mysterious future, we yet accept as part of our contemporary society.

Someone born in the Western world at the turn of the century has lived through changes that are so swift and violent we cannot comprehend them. They make the contrast between techno-logical advances and age-old suffering more brutal. People can receive heart transplants but they still die of starvation. The future is hurtling towards us, and yet it is no longer guaranteed. As we approach the millennium, all the old clichés of time (time running out, waiting for no man, just in time . . .) are invested with a new fear and with new literary possibilities. Writers may try to change or redeem the future before it actually happens – or the present as it is happening. Moving forwards into a near but anonymous future frees them from the strictures of realism and allows them to interpret the present through futurist eyes. It is the present in all its weirdness which is the alien landscape.

Some women writers certainly recognise the effect that the present culture of science-fiction strangeness has upon their imaginations and their sense of moral obligations. Elaine Feinstein considers that the ways in which she thinks about her world have recently changed, fundamentally affecting her writing. She has been 'pushed into the present' which, although not blacker than Europe in the 1940s ('nothing could be'), is 'much stranger'. And she sums up her sense of cultural alienation and urgency: 'the future has come to find us. All sorts of things that used to be in science fiction now happen. We are visiting our own future.'

Most of her novels are about how 'a woman copes with the kinds of things that come at her when she is on her own and embattled' and how a generation – Feinstein's own generation – is invaded by the sense that 'a lot of the things we take for granted have disappeared'. Internal and dreamy, these novels look back from the present to a past whose lessons of pain, though distant, reverberate in the present. But in the climate of the 1980s, which for Elaine Feinstein is haunted by the ghosts of the 1960s, darkened by the absolute horror of the Holocaust, and has at its feet the glow of apocalypse, she no longer finds it possible to write about the past in the lyrical and meditative style of her previous works. 'I just feel that I'm very much more up against it. I feel that what is going on in the world is out there, in the streets, and I absolutely can't ignore it. It all seems, well – pressing in on me.'

The sense of 'living in the future' was echoed by Emma Tennant, who goes one step further. Rather than recording what she sees, in the way that Margaret Drabble, Antonia Byatt or Elaine Feinstein do, she also acts as the prophet. She pointed out that the playful fantasies, comic apocalypses and satirical dystopias she has written in the past have an uncanny habit of becoming almost literal in the present. In *The Crack*, north and south are split in half and the south literally drifts off. In 1973 it could be read as a fanciful joke; in the late 1980s it reads more like an acute piece of political satire.

Emma Tennant thinks that futurism is now favoured by many writers because 'things are so peculiar'. There exists in late 1980s Britain, she says, a form of censorship which gives rise to the allegories and political concealments of futurism. For although we are still, largely, allowed to write things, 'we don't know how to – because it is all happening so fast and so bizarrely'. A writer is turning to dystopia because she wants the reader to 'believe' (in the sense of recognising the emotional or intellectual veracity) the writing. The present is not believable, and so the writer chooses to write about it indirectly. By using the devices and prophecies of futurism, she is 'sensing something in the air', 'picking something up in the ether before other people see it'.

While Emma Tennant gestured expansively towards the writer's often uncanny ability to 'sense something in the air', Maureen Duffy chooses to define the prophetic role of the writer more precisely. She called it 'the hypothesising imagination'. Although writing novels and poetry is for her a way of 'making sense of my internal life', she is a 'political animal' and so is always concerned with

> what a particular historical moment means and how it relates to what has gone before and will come after. I suppose that is what concerns me most of my day, and it is bound to come out in what I write. I look back or look forward in order to make sense of what is happening now – and also to predict in some sense what might happen.

She considers that the scientist's imagination and the artist's imagination, particularly the writer's imagination,

> use the same hypothesising faculties – and this is why writers so often get it right when they predict the future, although they only seem to be using their imagination. All the scientist does, after all, is to construct a hypothesis which can then be verified by experiment.

In some of her own fictions, the 'hypothesising imagination' constructs a scenario for a near future which is already, almost, the present – although drawn more sharply than we know it ourselves. *Gorsaga* is set in a bleak future Britain of unemployment, urban dereliction, riots, no-go areas and 'nons' – those unemployed people who have dropped through the net and are no longer treated or thought of as human. Into the nightmare landscape Gor is born; half-human, half-gorilla, he has been planned as an experiment, but escapes his capitivity to discover his origins and identity. Through the half-human Gor Maureen Duffy can explore the forces that destroy an individual. By looking at how man plays God and then condemns his experiments to live in a 'limbo on the edge of hell', she creates a parable of man's inhumanity in our terrible age of 'civilisation' and scientific advance. And she contrasts an animal's simple and honest emotions with our loss of emotional judgment.

Gorsaga is uncannily accurate about the future. Written in the early 1980s, many of its fictional events are now beginning to take place. Maureen Duffy described how she wrote the novel.

> I wanted to write about Gor and obviously I had to put him in a setting slightly ahead of our times because we had not, at that stage, combined humans with other primates. And so I drew a straight line, or series of straight lines, from the Thatcherite position in the early 1980s, chopped them off at a certain point, and placed Gor there. That is the world in which we now find ourselves. A world of inner-city decay and riots and homelessness. A world of water meters. I hope that I have exaggerated the cholera – but a world in which people are so poor they don't flush the toilet every time, bath once a week in the same water as each other, and so on. A world, therefore, of a general deterioration in health and the conditions of the poor. A world where you have the nons – who are the unemployed. A world of very high unemployment, where people virtually have to toss up to get jobs – which they then lose at the age of forty-five or fifty, and never get another. A world where men are supported by women's part-time labour. A world of the privatisation of buses. And yet, in contrast, a world in which you have the yuppies, the gentrification of areas like Fulham, the glorification of the country set.

The educational changes were also predicted in *Gorsaga*.
The thing, of course, which we haven't reached, is to say
'no representation without taxation' – the return to a
tax-based franchise. And the poll tax hints at that
possibility. That is the world I think we are in at the
moment.

Gorsaga is a fascinating example of the complex and time-
warping nature of much futurism. It prophesies the results of the
Thatcherite 1980s, but also acts as a comment and satire upon the
present we are occupying. Unlike Doris Lessing's *Canopus in
Argos* series, its strengths are not simply those of coherent social
and political theories and intelligent speculation. Maureen Duffy
constructs a possible and appalling future from the known
present, and then she places a group of individuals in her hypothetical and watertight structure whose emotional sufferings,
sexual desires and moral dilemmas are entirely familiar to us.
Such a strategy, which combines emotional familiarity with
futuristic strangeness, is quite different, too, from the utopia/
dystopia of Marge Piercy's *Woman on the Edge of Time*: there, the
characters have to be biologically modified in order to fit into
Piercy's scheme. And Duffy's emotional intensity and co-
mingling of the alien and familiar gives the novel the energy of
disjuncture. Moreover, like most of the compelling futurist
novels, its imaginative world is powerful enough to survive one
of futurism's frailties: that the future it attempts to predict will,
sooner or later, date the novel.

The preoccupations of *Gorsaga* are, however, similar to those
raised by Doris Lessing in many of her earlier novels, particularly in *The Four-Gated City* and *The Golden Notebook*, and by
Margaret Atwood in *The Handmaid's Tale*. What is humanity?
The half-human Gor, the dehumanised characters who inhabit
Lessing's urban dereliction or mingle in her Dantesque crowds,
Atwood's debased handmaid forced to incubate children not her
own, all contradict absolute definitions of humanity. And what
are true emotions? The social manipulation of human response
questions the existence of innate morality and instinct.

Such preoccupations are interesting in the context of gender. While it would be nonsense to suggest that women are always more interested in emotions than men, nevertheless they fequently do seem more fascinated by the *concept* of emotionality – how and why emotions operate. A futurist novel like Julian Barnes's *Staring at the Sun*, which depicts the effects of accelerating change and technological revolution, is more interesting for its portrayal of the near future than for his characters' behaviour within it. But the energy of *Gorsaga* comes from the intensely individual lives that operate against a political and social backcloth. The energy of *The Handmaid's Tale* comes from Margaret Atwood's anguished evocation of female suffering, and from her remembrance of the lost good things of life. The question posed is not simply, 'What is going to happen?' but, 'If this happens, how will we react and how will we feel?' What is being prophesied is not just a future, but the human consequences of that future.

The invention of optimism

While in Britain futurist novels predict a frightening twenty-first century, in countries where writers have experienced or witnessed state oppression they often write visions of a better future.

The novels by the South African author Nadine Gordimer range from the earlier explorations of individual lives in her country to the later more emphatically and explicitly political works. Her earlier writing is permeated by a suspicion of politics. They are humane and individualistic, looking at private relationships, both black and white, exploring tensions between adults and children, workers and bosses. With the brutal implementation of apartheid, however, and the horror of the Sharpeville massacre, she was forced into a new awareness that in a country where the private and public are particularly inseparable it is impossible to remain neutral. This theme is explicitly raised in her fourth novel, *The Late Bourgeois World*, in which a woman who is conscious of the errors, suspect motivations and impotence of the political groups around her realises that her well-argued, uncompromising inaction is no longer possible. History and politics invade every area of life.

With her growing political awareness, Nadine Gordimer's narratives are increasingly shaped by the history of her country. The politics of apartheid are no longer simply a force acting upon the individuals of her stories, they are the muscle and bone of her stories. In her short work *July's People*, she gives us a vision of a terrifying future. Evoking a post-revolutionary South Africa at the level of one particular family's experience, it has been read by many as a grim prophecy of what could happen in South Africa after a revolution. It is, in fact, a description of the interregnum in which civil war rages. Although Nadine Gordimer remains fascinated by the nuances of private relationships, ambiguities of human response, the collision or intertwining of sexual and political passions, this bitter dystopia about white South Africans' response to their loss of power has as its central character a country as much as a group of people.

A Sport of Nature is a startling contrast to *July's People*. Sliding without any change of tone from a social documentary-type novel to a theoretical kind of utopia, it predicts a near future in which Gordimer's beloved country attains majority rule. The 'sport' of the title is Hillela, a pretty white girl who, with her dependence on her good looks and shapely body, is a strange revolutionary heroine. Her development from wayward and adored young girl, whose ignorance borders on immorality in a country so bereft of illusions, to the wife of a black activist, mother and warrior, is the progress from passive innocence to active involvement. The unlikeliest person, Gordimer seems to be saying, can be effective.

A Sport of Nature is a highly theoretical book. At times its meticulous grounding in reality and in the bare facts of the past give it the air of dashing through history, with its intentions worn boldly on its sleeve. Such a sociological tone adds a strange sobriety to the passionate and triumphant dénouement. There is an unexpected chemistry at work in the intertwining of anger, resignation and insistent hope, which is paralleled by a strangely hybrid form. The novel is, simultaneously, realist, dystopian and utopian. Perhaps only a country so cruelly oppressed, violent, and laden with white inhumanity could produce such a merging of genres and tones. The futurism of the novel's conclusion seems no more unreal than the realism of its middle. The brutality with which Gordimer thrusts the facts of her country's history and present at us could, in another context, be satire. Here it is more akin to reportage.

What is striking, however, is that Nadine Gordimer can write a utopia out of a nightmare. From the blood, the horrors, the brutal deprivations, the individual and collective guilt of the whites, the necklace burnings, the detentions, the massacres, the relentless and inhumane oppression, she produces a vision of the future which is so hopeful that it seems like a gesture of defiant optimism rather than a prediction. A final statement – that 'the past is not a hunting, but was a preparation, put into use' – transforms the futurism of *A Sport of Nature*'s end into an exhortation: a piece of courageous rhetoric.

In times and places of oppression language can be the one affirmative gesture towards the future. Writers can create, out of horror, visions of a better world. Language then becomes the remaining and powerful instrument of defiance and survival, infinitely resilient because it feeds off and grows from the condition that is seeking to weaken it. Many of today's finest writers are writing in direct opposition to a system: the Latin American writers, the South African writers, the black American writers, the Eastern bloc writers. And many are writing fictions so passionate, forward-looking and undefeated that they challenge the European literature of individual pain, disillusion and despair. It is as if many white European and North American writers suffer from a cosmic guilt – a literary equivalent of original sin, which they attempt to expiate over and over again in their writings. Black and third-world writers, on the other hand, with their history of suffering, can seem fired rather than debilitated by their inheritance.

Most of the dystopias from North America or Britain are warnings: this is what the future might hold for us; this is what we, in our apathy, greed and individual complacency, might let

160

slip past us. But the magic realism of Latin America, the black American fictions that make history into the material of literature and take the whole world for their domains, are exhortations, resilient texts that offer some kind of belief both in the present and the future – they are acts of survival. Maya Angelou's exuberant tales of her own life pulse with a passionate commitment to living. Toni Morrison's stories of black lives in America bring humour, compassion and poetry to oppression, and her *Beloved* takes all the stuff of suffering – slavery, sexual abuse, the mother's loss of her children, poverty – and turns it into a fierce tribute. Gloria Naylor, after her first two realistic books about the contemporary lives of specific classes of black Americans, can step into the realms of fantasy with her triumphant *Mama Day*. She invents an alter-image of the white-dominated and racist Deep South by creating Willow Springs, an island which for 200 years has been owned and run by the blacks. Set in the future, with an upside-down history, it is a warm, buoyant and funny book. Nadine Gordimer can write a book that ends on a note of high hope, even as her own country is plunged into further brutality. Isabel Allende can write novels in which realism and fantasy criss-cross to produce histories of Chile's past and present – which are also visions of its future. Both *The House of the Spirits* and *Of Love and Shadows* combine personal witness with political and spiritual allegory – magical, certainly, but also grimly realistic. Angela Carter, standing out on the British literary landscape, can write novels whose extravagant and exotic surfaces and fabulously self-conscious theatricality turn away from the British literary tradition and use 'all of Western Europe as a great scrapyard'.

And these women, who use large canvasses and who combine myth with realism, history with futurism, are also reinforcing what is worth preserving in life. Large and abstract principles of freedom of action, speech and thought, of sexual and racial equality, of potential apocalypse, are flooded with the small and mundane events which make up our lives. Margaret Drabble's *The Radiant Way* or Michèle Roberts's *The Book of Mrs Noah*, for instance, are packed with descriptions of food and the rituals of mealtimes. The descriptions bring more than a sensuous delight to the·reader: amid the pictures of urban dereliction and 1980s malaise, or the stories of female oppression, they bring us back to the delights of ordinary and ignored everyday happiness. Similarly, the remembered acts of tenderness – wiping a child's nose, a kiss on the forehead – in Margaret Atwood's *The Handmaid's Tale* conjure up the delights we take for granted, not in an act of nostalgia, but with a repetitive and powerful insistence: that this is what we risk losing and this is what is worth preserving.

Such attention to detail and emotional minutiae, even in those novels of futurism and fantasy which grapple with grand issues and world events, occurs more frequently in women's writing. For women already write from the shadow side. They are already able, as marginalised beings, to experience the present as alien and to position themselves in the imagined landscapes of future, fantasy and myth in a less theoretical – and more 'realistic' – fashion.

That there are not more women in Britain whose work is both feminist and ambitious, concerned with small dense emotions and large world issues, does not imply a straightforward failure of the imagination and a loss of nerve. Feminism is young, perhaps only just emerging from its adolescence into maturity. Recent developments in female fiction – the new spirit of adventure, inclusion, diversity – suggests a more exciting literary future. Feminists are leaving home for the wider world.

CONCLUSION

Feminism, in its birth and development, has been largely writer-led. From Simone de Beauvoir and Kate Millett to Germaine Greer and Betty Friedan, from the French feminist critics to the practising novelists and poets, it has been reflected and inspired by writers' words and ideas. And in a generous symbiosis, the women's liberation movement has fed women's literature in general. It is hardly possible for a woman writing in the United States or Europe today not to be conscious of it or influenced by it. The culture in which, and of which, women write is a culture that feminism has helped to shape. One of the hopeful signs, as we approach the millennium, is that writers who are often depressed by the present and fearful for the future still insist upon the importance of their utterances. They still recognise the subversive power and imaginative possibilities of language.

The texts that writers produce need not simply reflect the spirit of the age with an abject realism – 'this is what our daily, worried life is like'. They can be active and resilient, refusing to be defined and confined by the times in which they are written. Many women's novels simply reiterate what we all feel we know already, and all know we have been told many times before – that life is tough, especially if you are female; that you have to struggle in order to find self-knowledge and an impure kind of happiness. They might be valuable in their analysis, but there is little sense of vision. The way in which such novels sink into their subjects can be dispiriting – as if the books themselves have become victims of their times. They are neither entering the mainstream, nor are they exploring interesting tributaries – rather, they are drifting, time-logged, in the shallows.

There have, however, been bold and transforming fictions in the 1980s which show the ways in which language can, in Grace Paley's determined words, be one of the 'horses that history rides' and not simply one of the carriages that it pulls. Such fictions rise above the introverted spirit of the times.

Sara Maitland pointed out how her profound anxiety about Britain's present and future affects the way that she writes in a powerful and unexpected way. She was appalled by the British general election of 1987, sensing that it marked a hardening of social attitudes.

> I was watching the telly when they declared the
> Walthamstow result. That had a big meaning for me,
> living here: it is where you go from here, on your first
> stage of having made it, and Walthamstow had been
> Labour ever since 1906. When they declared that the
> Conservatives had taken the seat I actually found myself
> thinking, 'This is a historic moment,' and bursting into
> tears. For what was happening was not that people were
> merely following their own interests – which is what East
> Enders have always done and always will – but were
> actually cutting the ladder off from other people. It was a
> very clear statement: 'We need the grindingly poor in
> order not to feel so badly off ourselves.' Those people
> who voted Conservative were the kids of old ladies living
> in tower blocks where the lift doesn't work.

The blunt horror that Sara Maitland felt in June 1987 was only an intensification of her general anxieties, which she experiences personally as a threat to her writing future ('I sometimes do fear that things are going to get so bad that I will not be able to justify spending my time writing'). But gloom does not have to produce a bleak, introverted kind of writing. For Sara Maitland the numbness of the early 1980s has given way to a willed positivism – 'every damn thing matters, and I'm not going to give in'.

She compares her writing in the 1970s with that of the late 1980s: their difference reverses expectations, and demonstrates how cultural pressures work in strange and devious ways upon the imagination of the writer.

> I wrote most of the stories in *Tales I Tell My Mother* at the end of the seventies. It was an extremely buoyant time for feminism – perhaps more for feminism than for any other cultural group. And they are all dire stories of warning and woe, perhaps because I'm such a prissy little moralist. I didn't sit down and think, 'Now the women's movement must be brought to a consciousness of its vices.' But, looking back on them, they are mostly short stories about limitations in women's aspirations for freedom – that we can't blame it all on forces outside; that our own errors will be more expensive in the long run than anything they can do to us.

A Book of Spells was written towards the end of the 1980s in a spurt of inexplicable creative energy and professional self-confidence.

> Almost half of them were written in the three months around Christmas 1986; it was one of the best times I ever had. I thought, 'Shit, I can do anything!' If someone rang me up tomorrow and wanted a short story about the life of a male sperm whale in the Pacific Ocean I'd think, 'Right, give me half an hour.' Out of everything that is worst about Thatcherism I wrote this incredibly buoyant book about exactly the reverse: about how the imaginative capacity in many women, and some men, can override the most appalling disasters.

The stories explicitly counter the materialism, philistinism and destructive apathy that Sara Maitland sees as characteristic of the

Thatcherite years. In them, and the indomitable power of the female imagination can pit itself against state indifference and cultural neglect. Literature need not simply reflect, respond to and react against its age; it can create its own alternative structure of spiritual and social values. It is in that sense that the 'new novel' can be newly subversive.

The 1980s have not been a decade which, in North America or Britain, has been conducive to literary 'flying'. On both sides of the Atlantic, editors' complaints about the lack of exciting and large-hearted contemporary novels testify to a decade of literary stagnation, illuminated here and there by a few books of out-standing stature. Many of the novels written by women, whether explicitly feminist or not, have been responsive and reflective. Their anxieties are often the small, personal, nagging ones so familiar within a constrained situation. And the writers' apparent inability or unwillingness to break free from their own time and place becomes itself a comment upon the insecure and insular age in which we live.

But there is an emerging refusal to succumb to the dispiriting climate of the 1980s. It is a refusal which has persuaded Mary Cunnane that we must call for 'passionate literature' from the 'hard times', made Gill Davies encourage 'impractical ideas' and forced Elaine Feinstein to 'hate' as well as fear what she sees happening around her.

And a few women, resisting the spirit of the age, have produced novels that, in the risks they take, the emotions they reveal and the largeness of their literary preoccupations, do 'fly' in the face of it. They absolutely refuse to succumb to the times in which they are written, and instead fire the grey stuff of daily life with passion and wide intelligence. Angela Carter's *Nights at the Circus* is a novel that, instead of being bogged down in the 1980s takes off from it. A huge cast of characters, a bizarre and compelling subject, a geography that takes us through Europe, from Paris and London to the cold wastes of Siberia, a generous time span, an audacious literary trick at the centre of the novel, an exotic and baroque prose, and a feminist roar of laughter that rips its way through the pages, all combine in a novel of enormous richness and breadth.

Carter takes her pick from literary traditions to make her own fictional form and world. She has written that she feels much more in common with certain third-world writers who, instead of 'instructing' people how to behave, as is common with many contemporary Western novels, 'are transforming fictional forms to both reflect and precipitate changes in the ways people feel about themselves – putting new wine in old bottles and, in some cases, old wine in new bottles'. She has also written that 'perhaps' what she wants to write are 'stories that could be read by guttering candlelight in the ruins of our cities and still give pleasure, still have meaning'. *Nights at the Circus* is a triumphant example of both comments – for it succeeds in transforming fictional forms, and it stands clear of the blinkered contemporaneity that limits many modern novels. Moreover, it has reached a larger audience than is traditionally expected for 'feminist' novels.

A novel published several years later than *Nights at the Circus*, *The Passion* by Jeanette Winterson, has an equivalent boldness of tone and largeness of theme. Set in the Napoleonic Wars and narrated by Henri, a sensitive man in militaristic times, and the Venetian Villanelle, who has webbed feet and has *literally* lost her heart to a married woman, *The Passion* is a fairytale about passion, gambling and androgynous ecstasy. It is set in France, Italy and Russia, and brims with a lovely sense of saga and language, an unashamed romanticism, and a sweeping eroticism. Although it is flawed by sloppy grammar and emotional clichés, it is exactly what Sara Maitland calls for, in her frustration with the 'brave' and small tale of individual lives.

The authors of these two novels write from different cultural inheritances – Angela Carter is a daughter of the 1960s and 1970s, Jeanette Winterson a child of the 1980s. Their view of the world, and the books that they write, are strikingly divergent. The characteristic that they nevertheless share is also shared by writers such as the North American Toni Morrison, Louise Erdrich and Gloria Naylor; the Latin American Isabel Allende; the South African Nadine Gordimer; the Canadian Margaret Atwood; the

New Zealanders Keri Hulme and Janet Frame. It is the boldness and breadth of their imaginations. They treat the world as their stage and language as a powerful instrument. They feel free to loot the literary past – and moreover most of them write fiction *as women writers*.

These are the writers who are truly entering the mainstream of literature and culture. Instead of inheriting a confined and stereotypic 'woman's world', they choose to treat the whole world as their own. By their bold and deliberate choice, they are not deserting feminism but are dramatically liberating the meaning of the 'feminist novel' – seeking to give it the implication of mainstream radicalism rather than fringe conservatism.

In a conversation published by Virago to celebrate their fifteenth year of publishing, the black North American writers Rosa Guy and Maya Angelou emphatically rejected introverted, self-concerned writing, and urged young writers to address themselves to the world around them:

> We are all victimised by the excesses, which are rapidly
> becoming the norm . . . we need our middle class, our
> young writers, to understand . . . The cries and screams
> . . . must be louder. Must be heard. We can no longer
> allow ourselves introspection about the days which were,
> we have to ready ourselves for the battle of days that are
> coming.

Angela Carter or Toni Morrison, Mary Gordon, Louise Erdrich or Sara Maitland might write *as women* and be liberated by their consciousness of gender. But there are many who write *as women* in a *self*-conscious, debilitating way. For them, it is as if feminism has become, simply, the form for their writing, which they obediently inhabit. And feminism, used in such a functional and preselective way, then closes the writer off from a larger world. Stereotypic feminist novels are disturbing precisely because they emphasise the ways in which self-conscious constraints come to dominate our perception of 'feminist' literature.

The perception of feminist writing as a strict and often puritanical alignment of political interests and aspirations tends to draw a sharp line between 'women's writing' and 'feminist writing' in a way that can be useful, but is more often crude and disturbing, since it dismisses the equivocal, questioning nature of many fictions. *Spare Rib*'s reviews, for example, tend to rate books by asking how feminist they are; they score, in other words, by being self-consciously correct rather than stimulating, politically interesting or even pleasurable. The magazine slips into the assumption that a book which offends the dictates of its particular feminist ideology is no longer a pleasure to read. On the other hand, *The Spectator*'s, or, under Auberon Waugh's editorship, *The Literary Review*'s book pages often display the flip side of such a response, sneering at ideological content as if it automatically disqualifies the book from being considered as 'art'. Both positions ignore the fictional, imaginative and troubling dimensions within novels, squeezing them into boxes of a different ideology: the stated or unstated ideology of the reviewer.

The common perception of 'feminist novels' cannot be entirely blamed on a distorting media. Critics are encouraged to perform their act of reduction because it has already been performed so well by some novelists. It is a crude exaggeration but also an accurate parody. Feminist writing is understood by many as a restrictive practice – an uncompromising but unsophisticated political discipline. And within such a reading, even apparently undisciplined pieces of autobiographical fiction lie cosily within the strict form of feminist self-awareness.

It is a form that can hobble the imagination. Of course, it is still true that women writers, especially if they are black or lesbian, and especially if they explicitly call themselves feminist, stumble against numerous obstacles not put in the way of men. But the internal barriers are more disturbing than these external, visible ones. Camouflaged, often unperceived, they can prevent women writers from speaking in their own voices. It is a crushing irony that feminism has always encouraged women to speak out and to write, but that feminist ideology can simultaneously curb female speech or confine it in an artificial dogmatism.

There is another version. To criticise the majority of feminist novels for their limited perspectives, ideological certitudes and individually concerned renderings of the world is to judge feminist literature by its negatives. If we shine the critical light from the opposite direction, then a different picture emerges. Most works of fiction have small ranges and short lives; there have never been more than a handful of novels in each generation whose relevance endures. From the near-vision of today, it might seem that feminist fiction has shrunk into a blinkered and cautious review of a drab modern culture. It will not look like that in twenty years time. Since the 1960s, many of the novels of stature have been written by women; of these, most have been either explicitly feminist or clearly informed by feminism. Looking back across the last few decades, with the distance that history provides, the angle of light falls less harshly upon the cultural landscape than it does today. It is not just that the outstanding figures upon it are often women, but that the contours of the ground on which they stand have been altered by feminism.

The achievements of women writers and, more specifically, of feminist writers, demonstrate that constraints can now be thrown off. Not only have figures such as Toni Morrison, Keri Hulme or Angela Carter written boldly imaginative works that plunder tradition and invent new female forms – they have also become popular writers. Their novels sell in large numbers and across large catchment areas. They have become 'mainstream' novelists not because of any conformity to an established and cautious literary tradition, but because their bold and disruptive texts have been widely read.

Moreover, the popular potential of ambitious feminist fiction is becoming increasingly recognised. In 1988 Maureen Duffy's intelligent and imaginatively powerful futuristic novel *Gorsaga* was made into a television film series which starred Charles Dance, and the rights to Mona Simpson's epic account of a mother–daughter relationship *Anywhere But Here* were bought by Disney. In the preceding few years, Angela Carter's fairy-tale subversion *The Company of Wolves*, Jane Rule's lesbian love story

The Desert of the Heart and Alice Walker's extraordinary *The Color Purple* were all screened and reached large cinema audiences. As such examples demonstrate, we already have our mothers of the novel, and our examples of passionate and enduring feminist fiction; the groundwork has been laid for dramatic and original feminist writing. The question now to be asked is not merely, 'What are they, the female authors, ready to write?' but, 'What are we, the audience, ready to read?' With the introduction of that second question, dissatisfaction with feminist literature shifts and is broken up. It challenges the readers, as well as the writers, demanding of us, too, imagination and passion and readiness.

When writers such as Toni Morrison or Angela Carter maintain their explicit feminism but divest it of narrow self-consciousness, they smash our expectations and demonstrate once again the imaginative possibilities of feminism *as a process* involving both the writer and the reader. It is a process which possesses the power to transform the world and all its fictions.

There are signs that, out of the imaginative hiatus and cultural apathy of the consumer decade, a newly adventurous women's writing is emerging. It is as if some women writers have endured the drab days for long enough, and as if an increasing number of readers are ready for their creative renaissance. For a handful of women are beginning to write big novels that use literary and historical pasts to reflect the state of a nation, and to prophesy the future – novels, moreover, that resonate with a moral urgency. Their writers believe they have something important to say to us about the way we are living today, and the way we might find ourselves living soon. They give us the sense that now is history after all, and that each particular moment resonates with its surrounding past and future. By fusing imagination and reality, they demonstrate that literature can discover and, by discovery, change our worlds. If we let it.

INDEX

INDEX